ALAN RAE was a long-serving employee of H____ in the team's dugout on match days. Part-tim____ Edinburgh Royal Infirmary, he later joined th____ well-respected member of the off-pitch team, and throughout the____ eight managers, three owners and numerous players come and go. Alan left Hearts in 2005 after 23 years at Tynecastle Stadium. He now lives in the Scottish Borders.

PAUL KIDDIE began his journalistic career with DC Thomson in Dundee in 1984, where he spent twelve years before joining the *Edinburgh Evening News* sports desk. A similar length of service with Scotsman Publications saw him report on Hearts for six tumultuous seasons, during which time he first met Alan Rae. After a year living in the USA, Paul was offered the chance to return to Scotland as communications Manager at Heart of Midlothian FC, a position he took up in January 2007.

From the brink of possible collapse to the arrival of Vladimir Romanov, most fans of football will find something of interest in this book. SCOTTISH FITBA

Rae's wealth of medical knowledge is evident in the book, and his psychological insight into the players he treated is also much to the fore...the book is above all a modern history of Hearts. THE SCOTSMAN

Football-wise, Alan Rae was the best physio I ever worked with. He was second to none and other physios even came to him to ask for advice. He brought a real professional approach to the physiotherapy side of things at Hearts and was a real gentleman as well. WALTER KIDD

I remember coming back to Tynecastle after breaking a leg in Majorca and doing my ankle pretty seriously. He got things healed up pretty quickly using the good old fashioned methods and my fitness test before my last game for Hearts involved jumping on a trampete three or four times on my dodgy ankle! Alan told me if it felt alright, that was fine, I'd play. It was still pretty sore but he strapped me up, and I scored the winner against Dunfermline at Tynecastle – and then Dick Advocaat put in a £2 million bid for me so Alan must have known what he was doing! He was always very straight with players and was a great guy to have at the club. I had a lot of time for Alan and as all good physios should be, outwith all the medical side of things, he was brilliant in the dressing room. It's so important for someone in his position to have a good relationship with the players and in my time at Hearts Alan was brilliant. NEIL MCCANN

Alan was a fantastic physio and fantastic for the young boys. When it came to the discipline side of things, there was no one better than Alan and that stood them all in good stead for when they progressed. It's something you don't normally associate with a physio but they knew what he was about and feared if they didn't do a job properly, they could be there all night. He was a one-off, a bit eccentric but a top guy and a fantastic character. JIM JEFFERIES

Alan Rae was a top man for me, a fantastic person and not just from the physio side. When I came to the club as a 16-year-old straight from school he helped me settle in and turned me into a man. He never just gave treatment, he taught me how to apply myself away from the football, the way to dress, the way to turn up for work, etc. The ground staff back then was a lot different to now as they all had to do the crap jobs and Alan kept me on my toes and wasn't shy in telling me I had done something wrong. He was just fantastic for our development as people not just players. In my time as a player I had a really bad injury and there were times when I would get quite low, but he was a massive influence, always there encouraging me and he got me back quicker than I maybe should have. I can't speak highly enough of him as he saved my career when I was just 20 years old. His patter was horrendous, though! GARY LOCKE

When I first came back to Hearts they didn't have a full-time physio – Alan was the physio but he worked at the Royal Infirmary – and I found that bizarre for a club of Hearts' stature. If you wanted treatment you had to go to the Infirmary and Alan would see you in his lunch break! That continued for a couple of years until he turned full-time. He didn't suffer fools gladly. He had the youngsters organising things to within an inch of their lives, while having a great relationship with the senior players. I had nothing but the highest respect for him. He did have a 'mental' side to him when he could explode at a youngster for asking a daft question. EAMONN BANNON

Alan was really good at his job, was loyal to every manager at the club and was brilliant for Hearts. Every time I think of him I recall a story from a break at Christmas time when we went to Marbella when I was manager. George McNeil and Bert Logan were there and we were out for a few beers when Alan for some unknown reason decided to climb a tree and raced up it like a monkey! He came back down and just started laughing and that summed him up for me – he was very professional but had a jovial side to his character when he would come away with the unexpected. SANDY CLARK

The physios never dictated to the gaffer, he told them he wanted the players fit. And Alan knew his job really well. I thought he was great and he had a terrific manner with the players. He brought a bit of discipline to the younger ones and you definitely didn't want to walk into his room uninvited or you'd get short shrift. People might have taken him the wrong way but he was a good character who cared for his players. Even if he was a bit of a nutcase! STEVE FULTON

He wouldn't do anything before his coffee break first thing in the morning! He was an absolutely fantastic physio who even though he worked in a tiny little physio room at Tynecastle got people back from injury very quickly. A wonderful man with a very dry sense of humour who was brilliant company. ALLAN PRESTON

Alan was the best physio I worked with in my career, without a shadow of a doubt, and I was shocked when he left Hearts as I thought he would have been there for ever. SCOTT CRABBE

He was one of the most trustworthy, wonderful, lunatic, crazy, loveable, straight-jacketed men I have ever met in my life. JOHN ROBERTSON

Hands on Hearts
A Physio's Tale

ALAN RAE

with Paul Kiddie

Luath Press Limited

EDINBURGH

www.luath.co.uk

First published 2011
This edition 2012

ISBN: 978 1 908373 54 0

The authors' right to be identified as authors of this book under the Copyright,
Designs and Patents Act 1988 has been asserted.

The paper used in this book is recyclable. It is made from low-chlorine pulps
produced in a low energy, low emissions manner from renewable forests.

Printed and bound by
Martins the Printers, Berwick upon Tweed

Typeset in 11 point Sabon

To my wife Sheila and my family – Frances, Helen,
Christine and Neil – who all suffered for the cause.
Alan Rae

To Margaret for the wonderful job she does as a wife and mother,
and to Caitlin and Michael for their love and laughter.
Paul Kiddie

Contents

Acknowledgements

While writing this series of recollections I received help and information from many former players who gave their time generously. The book itself would have remained a notion but for the able assistance of Paul Kiddie who has worked well beyond what any reasonable person would put up with. All or nothing must be his motto. For his commitment alone I hope this book has some modest success not least because a proportion of the proceeds will be donated to the Sick Children's Hospital, Edinburgh.

I wish to thank Gavin MacDougall at Luath, who chose to take a punt on *Hands on Hearts* and my editor Jennie Renton, who slapped the text into shape and yours truly along with it, metaphorically of course. My gratitude to Gavin, Jennie and the staff at Luath pales to 'a daimen icker in a thrave' in terms of their assistance.

A man for whom I have great respect read the text prior to publication; Pilmar Smith, the former vice chairman of Heart of Midlothian, who had almost a monopoly on common sense during his tenure at Tynecastle and still retains this faculty. A former director of the club, James Clydesdale, was largely responsible for making my side of Tynecastle habitable and also kindly advised me on the chronology of the stadium reconstruction.

Many of the photographs in this book (accompanying my own) are the gift of Eric McCowat. I thank him for this huge contribution from his Sports Photo Archive which has so enriched the visual aspect of this book. I'd also like to thank Scotsman Publications Ltd for kindly allowing me access to their archive.

Mr Craig Levein needs no introduction from me. In his Foreword he has written more than a few words about his time at Tynecastle as player and manager. His reflections on my state of mind echo the notion that you don't have to be mad to work at Tynecastle, but it sure helps. Thank you, Craig, for your support in this project.

When searching for dates, scores and names, the London Hearts website and Norrie Price's fine book, *Gritty, Gallant and Glorious*, proved invaluable. I would recommend both to all dedicated Hearts supporters.

I am grateful to Heart of Midlothian FC for kindly allowing the club badge to be used on the cover of this book.

Finally, I must thank my wife Sheila and the family, who encouraged me throughout this undertaking and helped by reading through material and criticising when the text got out of hand.

Foreword by Craig Levein

When I first started at Hearts in 1983, Alan Rae was full-time at the Royal Infirmary and did his work with the players on a part-time basis. The injured ones would have to jump in their cars at lunchtime and drive to the hospital to get treatment during his lunch break – and he was looking after just about all the squad at the time.

I probably spent more time with him than anyone else at the club and that is why nowadays I question my sanity! I maybe spent more time with him over a long period than I did my team-mates. He was as mad as a hatter, completely nuts, but a man for whom I have huge admiration.

Quickly becoming the club's full-time physio, he wasn't someone who allowed you to feel sorry for yourself and that was something which benefited me with my history of knee injuries. He was good at setting small goals so that I could focus on something in the near future rather than think, shit, I'm out for a year. He would set these little targets to help make me feel I had achieved something in a short space of time and for me that was a much better approach.

I have an awful lot of time for Alan, who was very supportive when I was injured. I have always had a lot of respect for him and I think he respected the fact I'd had a lot of setbacks. He was an extremely fair person with everyone and didn't have favourites – he went off his head at all of us! He had his quirks and it wouldn't take much to set him off and it wouldn't be the first time I have seen a bottle of talc bounce off someone's head!

Part of physiotherapy is psychology and keeping players focused, and he was really good at that while maintaining a bit of fun as well – we used to have some great laughs, mostly at Kevin Thomas' expense who was in there for a while!

He was a hard taskmaster and not very tolerant of people not doing their work properly, which I think is a great thing. If you want to come back better than ever from an injury you have to be focused on doing your rehab properly.

Our relationship was quite close because I had been in his room for what must have been around three years altogether and we got to know each other quite well. It was almost like a marriage as such – we were comfortable even with silence and when I became manager of

Hearts it didn't change that much.

The absolute trust I had in him meant that when I was manager I knew he could take charge of situations and he didn't need me breathing down his neck asking questions all the time. I would let him dictate the rehab and tell me when people were going to be fit. Some previous managers would be at him all the time telling him they need so and so fit, whereas I knew Alan was doing everything he could to get players back fit as quickly as possible.

As a manager you take immense comfort from people around you doing their job properly, you want to feel secure, they are all thinking the same way and focused on the same goals. I didn't need to worry about Alan on that score so he became part of the backroom team along with Peter Houston and John McGlynn. When I came back to the club as manager it was like stepping back into an old set of slippers – it was comfortable for me to have Alan as the physio and I trusted him completely as I knew he was the best man for the job, that he understood the demands on a manager, and that allowed me to get on with my job which was hard enough without worrying about anything else.

His humour was off the wall but for me it was the unpredictability of his explosions. One such occasion happened when we were in getting treatment and someone conducting a stadium tour opened the door and came right through with a bunch of school kids and up towards the gym. He had this incredulous look on his face as if to say: 'Where the **** are they going?' They were just kids but as the last one disappeared out the door to go up to the gym, they left it open. Alan looked at me with his usual deadpan expression and said, 'Excuse me a second,' walked over to the door, grabbed it and shouted after them: 'Were you born in a f****** barn!" before slamming it shut and turning round and coming back as if nothing had happened. On pre season tours he would do his work but was then a bit like a tourist either wandering around doing his own thing or photographing stuff – some of his efforts you will see later in the book.

At times I felt he got taken for granted with an enormous work load and consequently he was unable to have a normal family life. His durability and stamina shone through as what he did was above and beyond the call of duty and Heart of Midlothian Football Club owes Alan Rae a huge debt of gratitude.

Preface

I have always enjoyed the challenge of fresh circumstances. Practising physiotherapy had taken me round the globe in the years before I came to Hearts and I had become adept at coping with change, which was just as well. For the next 23 years – years that saw momentous changes at the Hearts – I worked under three owners and eight managers, all of whom put their own stamp on the continuing development of the club. The following chapters will jog some memories, not all happy, of the period 1982 to 2005, when I was fortunate enough to practise my clinical skills as a physiotherapist at Tynecastle where I came to know, players from youth level to the first team at Heart of Midlothian FC.

Alan Rae, September 2011

Chronology

1982	In June Alan Rae is invited to provide physiotherapy services for Heart of Midlothian.
1982–83	Alex MacDonald and Sandy Jardine guide Hearts to promotion into the Premier League.
1983–84	After five straight league wins at the start of this season Hearts qualify for Europe.
1984–85	Hearts play Paris Saint-Germain and comfortably stave off the memory of recent relegations.
1985–86	Hearts beaten by Glasgow Celtic on goal difference for the league title and lose the Scottish Cup Final to Aberdeen.
1986–87	Hearts lose narrowly to Dukla Prague, Wayne Foster making his European debut by scoring first in the home leg. On 31 October Craig Levein is seriously injured in a reserve match at Easter Road.
1987–88	End of season league position, second behind Celtic, guarantees European football at Tynecastle in the next season.
1988–89	John Robertson sold to Newcastle in April 1988, Iain Ferguson signed as replacement in July 1988. Joint manager Sandy Jardine sacked in October 1988. Bayern Munich play at Tynecastle in February 1989 in the UEFA Cup quarter-final. John Robertson re-signed in December 1988.
1989–90	In March 1990 Hearts lose by 4-1 at Pittodrie in Scottish Cup. Alan Rae joins Hearts on a full-time basis in January 1990.
1990–91	After a poor pre-season and a losing start in the league, Alex MacDonald and Walter Borthwick are sacked in November 1990. Fine victory v Dnepr. 1-1 away and 3-1 at home. Craig Levein and Dave McPherson play in the World Cup finals. Joe Jordan and Frank Connor are appointed as manager and assistant manager in September 1990.
1991–92	Joe and Frank split the Old Firm. Hearts second in league behind Rangers. Ian Baird signed in July 1991 and Glynn Snodin signed in March 1992.
1992–93	Hearts' youth policy pays off: Youths win prestigious BP Cup against Rangers at Ibrox.

After an unlucky loss in the cup semi-final and losing 6-0 at Falkirk on 1 May 1993, Joe and Frank are sacked.

Sandy Clark manages the team until the end of the season.

1993–94   Sandy Clark and Hugh McCann are appointed as manager and assistant manager.

Justin Fashanu is signed in July 1993.

Hearts play Atlético Madrid in September 1993.

Wallace Mercer sells Heart of Midlothian to Chris Robinson and Leslie Deans who take over in June 1994.

Clark and McCann sacked. Vice chairman Pilmar Smith leaves.

1994–95   Tommy McLean and Tom Forsyth are appointed as manager and first team coach in June 1994.

Eamonn Bannon is appointed assistant manager, Walter Kidd becomes youth coach in July 1994.

Wheeling and dealing after the loss of McLaren and McKinlay. In come Cramb, McPherson, Miller, Nelson, Jamieson, Hagen and Hamilton.

Hearts beat Rangers in Scottish Cup quarter-final at Tynecastle but lose 0-1 to Airdrie in the semi-final at Hampden on 8 April 1995.

Relegation is avoided on 13 May 1995, the last day of the season, in a victory against Motherwell at Tynecastle.

McLean and Forsyth leave the club in July 1995.

1995–96   Jim Jefferies and Billy Brown are appointed as manager and assistant manager in August 1995.

Rousset, Bruno and Eskilsson signed.

Hearts reach Scottish Cup Final in May 1996.

Captain Gary Locke seriously injured as his team is soundly beaten by Glasgow Rangers.

1996–97   Steady improvement of the team – Bruno, Pointon, Cameron, Weir, Fulton and Rousset steady the ship.

Rangers again the opponents in the Scottish League Cup Final in November 1996.

Locke returns to fitness in January 1997 after six months' rehab.

1997–98   After three home ties and a semi-final at Ibrox against Falkirk, Hearts reach the Scottish Cup Final, once more against Rangers.

A Fifer and a Frenchman seal the first cup victory since 1956.

1998–99   Steven Pressley is signed.

A resurgence in the final quarter of the season sees the team pull away from relegation zone.

1999–2000	A much improved Hearts side qualifies for Europe and clinches third spot in the league.
2000–01	Popular Rousset loses his place to Antti Niemi.
	Hearts are unlucky to lose on away goals to Stuttgart.
	Disaster at Easter Road in October 2000 where the team lose six goals to their arch rivals, Hibs.
	Jefferies leaves the club in November 2000.
	Craig Levein is appointed manager in December 2000.
2001–02	Shrewd signings Alan Maybury, Kevin McKenna, Ricardo Fuller and Austin McCann stabilise the team.
	Steven Pressley rising to prominence.
2002–03	Under Levein's guidance Hearts reach third place in the SPL.
	Phil Stamp is signed.
2003–04	A comfortable win in a preliminary round against Bosnian opposition takes Hearts into the second round of the UEFA Cup.
	Despite a fine 1-0 victory in the away leg, Bordeaux win at Tynecastle on 27 November 2003.
	Consistency in the SPL again secures third spot in the table.
	Hearts move to the new Soccer Academy at the Heriot-Watt Riccarton campus in May 2004.
2004–05	Pre-season training in Vancouver.
	Andrew Driver makes a brief appearance in friendly match.
	A home win against Braga in the UEFA Cup at Murrayfield followed by an away leg draw takes Hearts into the league sections of the competition.
	Levein's managerial credentials soar and he leaves for Leicester in October 2004.
	Enter Hearts legend John Robertson as replacement manager with Donald Park as his assistant.
	Robinson sells Hearts to Vladimir Romanov in December 2004.
	Alan Rae contemplates end game.
	Robbo and Parkie leave – scunnered – in May 2005.
	Youth team coach John McGlynn and former player Stephen Frail take control until end of season.
2005–06	George Burley is appointed as manager.
	During a pre-season match in Dublin against St Patrick's, Graham Weir sustains a leg fracture.
	League season starts well.
	Alan Rae leaves after a home match against Motherwell.

CHAPTER I

Kicking Off

IN ALEX MACDONALD'S COMPANY I once ventured, 'When I played...' A moment's uneasy silence, then the Hearts manager said: 'You never played!' After that rebuke, when in professionals' company, I have always listened without comment. Clearly, some care has to be taken here when I write about my own modest experiences on the football field.

My uncle, a useful inside forward playing in the summer amateur leagues, took me to watch Queen of the South when I was a lad growing up in Lockerbie. Applegarth, Kinnel Rovers, Kettleholm and Hoddam Rangers (who paradoxically wore green hoops) were the teams I followed. In my teens I turned out for youth and local amateur sides and later for a works' team in Renfrew, and, for a season, for Gala Rovers. Football was the game I watched and *tried* to play. Marriage, children and work put paid to both.

In 1962 I enrolled at Tom McClurg Anderson's Scottish School of Physiotherapy. Physiotherapists for many UK teams qualified here, including the pioneering Tom McNiven, who became the pathfinder for physios who wanted to get involved in professional football. From Third Lanark, a club which was strong in the early '60s, he moved on to Hibernian, where his talents were recognised by the Scotland team manager. In his wake came Ronnie McKenzie, John Watson, Eric Ferguson, Jim McGregor, Tom Craig, Ricky McFarlane, Neil Falconer and Bill Shearer, all products of Anderson's School.

In mid-July 1982 I received a phone call from an old school friend, Jim Donaldson, who told me that Sandy Jardine was leaving Rangers to join Hearts as a player, but also to assist his player-manager buddy, and that he was looking for a physiotherapist. I took the job, reasoning that I could combine following the game with expanding my clinical knowledge. I had been working outside Scotland for many years and when I came to Edinburgh in 1979 I was not particularly familiar with Scottish professional football. All that was about to change.

On my first visit to Tynecastle I was staggered by the state of the place. The ground was under-maintained and everything looked shabby, including the physio room, which appeared to multi-function as a laundry room (if an old bath full of dirty kit was anything to go by), a temporary dormitory for the ground staff and a canteen. Just where clinical treatments were carried out was anybody's guess. And as I would soon discover, when kit was being handed out, the devil took the hindmost.

On one occasion shortly after starting in the job, I saw a lad, after washing the floors, proceed to suck up the excess water with a vacuum cleaner. It was not unknown for bath towels to be used for generally rearranging the dirt and cleaning boots. There was one washing machine and one dryer in the place, and laundry was often suspended on ropes under the grandstand to dry. However I should mention here that all the other grounds I visited around that time were every bit as bad as Tynecastle.

Willie Montgomery, the groundsman, didn't suffer fools but was quite gentle, at least in footballing terms, with the young lads who acted as ground staff. I liked him. He had served his time at one of the esteemed golf courses in the capital and was a source of many anecdotes.

During cold spells, when the covers had to be pulled over the playing surface, it was all hands to the pumps and it was hard work for the youngsters. No gloves, no tracksuits, they pulled the sheets on and off. Willie would roar: 'Pull!'

The reply: 'Wur pullin', Wullie.'

Willie's disdainful retort: 'Pull? Ye couldnae pull a sodger aff yer sister!'

On the positive side, everyone I met at Hearts was helpful and keen to have someone around who at least knew some first aid.

Alex MacDonald was going into his second season as player-manager and Sandy and he were very much on the same wavelength. Walter Borthwick was the team coach and it wasn't long before John Binnie was recruited to look after the reserves and part-time playing staff. Walter and John were especially helpful to me, someone who was totally ignorant of the *professional* game.

Wallace Mercer, the chairman, who needs no introduction, had taken over this ailing club, supported by two dedicated Hearts men, Les Porteous and Pilmar Smith. In the background was former chairman and player, Bobby Parker, whose great depth of inside track was invaluable to the club.

The Hearts team was a blend of youth and experience. David Bowman, Gary Mackay, John Robertson and Ian Westwater were to become top class Premier League performers. Henry Smith, Roddy McDonald, Paddy Byrne and Stewart McLaren were seasoned professionals, as was prolific goal-scorer Willie Pettigrew. Playing alongside Willie was Gerry McCoy, with Peter Marinello as a wide man (winger). In the First Division that year, Airdrie, Partick Thistle, Falkirk and St Johnstone would all be competing for the two promotion places, their campaigns underpinned by home grounds that were uninviting as far as the opposition was concerned. I discovered that many people associated with Hearts were pessimistic regarding the club's future. Pilmar Smith, a self-made man, was dismissive of the doom merchants: 'Ravers, out and out ravers,' he would say in his own inimitable fashion. 'Hearts will always survive!'

An East of Scotland Shield tie at Easter Road was the venue for my first match as physiotherapist. I couldn't have got off to a worse start. I realised I had forgotten to pack the treatment hamper and confessed to Alex while he was having his pre-match shower. He took this in his stride, as he did with most things in football. Needless to say, the round trip to collect it was completed in an embarrassed blur. The home side won the match, scoring with a rebound off Hibernian star defender Jackie McNamara's back. One of my lasting memories is being showered with grit thrown from the home dugout by Pat Quinn, no less. Perhaps he picked up this stunt from his days at his junior club, Bridgeton Waverley.

The League Cup campaign started with an away match against Motherwell. It was a hot afternoon with the home team shading it 3-2, Hearts undone by a late Alfie Conn Jnr goal. Derek O'Connor kept Hearts in the match with a back post volley. A part-time player who had been in and out of the team, Derek had played for other clubs but he was always Hearts-daft. Rumour had it that he failed to turn up for his current club some Saturdays as he preferred to watch his beloved Jambos at home.

In the dressing room after the final whistle, I looked around at the players as they sat there totally drained; no injuries, but wiped out. I realised that it was going be my role to help them cope not just with the physical but with the mental and social impacts of the professional game. Many of the attributes of players are overlooked by lay people and I found it illuminating when the management and coaches pointed out to me how moves and techniques were performed. But I kept it firmly in mind that my own focus was how to get these guys out onto the field of play in as good shape as possible.

Pre-season 83–84 official photograph. Back row: Donald Park, David Bowman, Alan Redpath, Stuart Gauld, Stuart Dall, Roddie McDonald, Paul Cherry, Malcolm Murray, Neil Irving, Derek O'Connor, Gary Mackay. Middle Row: Walter Borthwick (first team coach), John Binnie (reserve team coach), Jimmy Bone, Paddy Neilson, Willie Pettigrew, John Brough, Henry Smith, Ian Westwater, Stewart MacLaren, Jimmy Sandison, Willie Johnston, Alan Rae (physiotherapist). Front Row: Alex MacDonald (player/manager), Mark Tomassi, Peter Shields, Gerry McCoy, Walter Kidd (captain), Gary Sutherland, George Cowie, Colin Scott, John Robertson, Peter Finlay and Sandy Jardine (assistant manager/player).

Many of the techniques I had learned had lain dormant when I was working in other fields of physiotherapy. Now I was applying them and I soon appreciated their efficacy. The use of strappings became of paramount importance when working with a small first team squad. By laying adhesive tape supportively on the skin, the underlying nerve endings transferred 'stretch' impulses to muscles, enabling them to react quicker over damaged joints. As a student I had gained work experience with Clydebank Juveniles, which now proved invaluable as I set about developing my working practice, as did the attitude and example of Bill McIntyre and Jimmy Strang, who ran these teams with total commitment to nurturing young talent.

The first leg of the quarter-final of the League Cup was played on 27 October against John Greig's Rangers at Ibrox. David Bowman was given the task of marking Jim Bett, a fine attacking midfield player. This ploy frustrated Rangers. With ten minutes left, a wide right player by the name of John McDonald was introduced. He ran with a peculiar gait, as though his legs were not a pair, but he proved too much for a tired defence. Rangers won 2-0.

At Firhill a nervy point was gained, although Airdrie ensured that vital share of the spoils was soon forgotten when they ran out 5-2 winners at Tynecastle. But even with results like these, Bobby Parker was reassuring. He had seen it all before – many times!

Hand ball in the box from Hearts left back Peter Shields early in the return leg semi against Rangers gave Hearts a mountain to climb, and when Derek Johnstone scored late on the Glasgow outfit progressed on an aggregate 4-1 score.

Nevertheless, Hearts had shown what they were capable of doing against three top flight sides over six games. The drama continued to unfold with Hearts returning pointless from three games in Fife, two against Raith and one against Dunfermline, the cruel nature of these defeats making them all the more difficult to accept.

On a snowy night at East End Park, Dunfermline, with the final whistle about to be blown, scored with the last kick of the ball. On 29 March, in the second game against Raith Rovers, the lean and wiry Hearts full back Stuart Gauld – aka 'Bamber' – was hit on the forearm at Stark's Park. His upper limb was glued to his side – ball to hand – to this observer. Not so, as far as the referee was concerned. He deemed it 'hand to ball' and awarded a clinching penalty.

Life at Hearts was nothing if not a steep learning curve. At home to East Fife in a Scottish Cup tie, left back Peter Shields hurt his wrist and without any thought as to the consequences of his not being on the park, I helped him to the sidelines to tape things up. No sooner had I started to work on him than the opposition exploited the positional hole left by Peter and scored! In those days, depending on the referee, a player could be treated on the park and didn't have to go to the side and await a summons to re-enter play. After that incident, you can be sure that I made the player stay on until I was expressly ordered to remove him.

The Tynecastle faithful were beginning to realise this was a different Hearts outfit to those of the recent past. The return of decent crowds began, but it was a slow transition. Dynamo Kiev, with Oleg Blokhin and Vadym Yevtushenko on board, came to play a friendly. Only 3,000 fans turned up to watch these world-class players strut their stuff.

St Johnstone were the visitors for the New Year fixture and, not for the first time, the Hearts fans raised a glass to toast the skills of Henry Smith in goal. After a fabulous save from John Brogan at the School End, Hearts went on to win, with Pettigrew finishing at the near post from Paddy Byrne's cross. The vast majority of the 17,000 crowd made their way home in optimistic mood; 1983 had started well.

When I got to know Frank Connor, a man of many football managerial positions, he told me that the false faces came off after the New Year. Well, Frank did tend to speak in parables and metaphors. I think he meant that the genuine articles shone through in the second half of the season. Not that I would have known at that stage.

After scoring at Broomfield in the festive period, Pettigrew went strangely off the boil and it was then that the signing legacy of Bobby Moncur (Hearts manager 1980–81) bore fruit. Young Gary Mackay had been playing regularly, as had David Bowman. David was mature for his years. He looked and played like a fully grown adult and had probably been allowed to play with conditions which are nowadays better recognised: rapid development can mean that the muscles are stronger than their bony attachments and this can lead to injuries involving the growing bone. Gary developed at a slower pace, which paid off – he went on to play a record number of games for the club. Also signed by Moncur, John Robertson, who had been waiting patiently in the wings, now stepped up to play alongside Dangerous Derek.

Ian Brown, a former Hearts coach, tells of a second-half performance by JR, aged 15, against Morton at Cappielow in a cup-tie.

With Hearts 2-0 down at half time, the team talk went along the lines of: 'A bit more from you, wee man.'

'Ah'm here tae score goals,' was the retort.

'Well, what's the score the noo?'

Out JR went and bagged a hat-trick, with Derek O'Connor completing the total.

The vital points won from promotion rivals St Johnstone and Airdrie, three and four respectively, were crucial (at that time two points were given for a win) and put further distance between Hearts and league rivals Raith and Dunfermline. They did not prosper at Tynecastle, neither did Partick or Ayr, and these clubs were soon out of contention.

On a fine Saturday at Muirton Park in Perth, St Johnstone hosted what was to be the First Division title decider. Hearts arrived with a huge support from the Gorgie Boys (and Girls). In a tight game the winner came from Raymond Blair who scored with a header at the back post: 2-1 Saints, Davie Bowman's goal not enough on the day. Saints stayed top of the league, leaving Hearts in need of two points to secure second place and promotion. It seemed as if visiting teams upped their game when at Tynecastle while the good Hearts following at away matches created an atmosphere which often lifted the *home* side.

The penultimate game, against Dumbarton at Boghead, saw a young JR end the game as a contest in the first half: 4-0 was the final score, Gary and Derek adding to Robbo's brace. Promotion was secured.

Alex and Sandy's blend of experience and professionalism had raised the club to where it should be. The days of a player selling Mars

Bars in a dressing room booming with disco music were over.

The next season would be a test for both these ex-Rangers men. Alex had been, and still tried to be, a 'box to box' player. Clearly possessing a 'big engine', his resting pulse rate would have been in the low 40s or high 30s; he brought to my mind the Olympic 10,000 metres runner Brendan Foster. Sandy, on the other hand, was the 'class horse', quick enough in his prime to catch pigeons. He also had a harder line in his approach to his team-mates, while Alex was more guarded.

Earlier in the season Fifer Willie Johnston had been recruited, which meant that three European trophy winners were reunited, albeit a little older and wiser. That's not to say they got on any better with match officials. Willie was sent off against Celtic in the Scottish Cup while Alex got his marching orders against Ayr United in a league match at Somerset Park on a very windy Saturday. Sandy Jardine was not as easily roused.

Off the field, Willie was quiet and laconic. Not so on the field: he was an explosive winger who would not be put upon. The fact that he had previously worked down the pit caused me to recall a lecture at the Scottish School of Physiotherapy by a visiting clinician, who said that the left-sided Rangers wing half Jim Baxter derived his poise and balance from having worked in confined spaces at the coal face, an anecdote which I took with a liberal amount of salt.

Alex MacDonald trusted his players and they him. As a result, they would play with injuries heavily strapped. If the player couldn't train, Alex would leave them to recover without any badgering. A player he could trust and who was willing would be better than any uninjured replacement.

To get players as fit as possible, Sandy Jardine's contacts in Edinburgh were tapped. Scotland's greatest-ever boxer, Ken Buchanan, introduced the squad to skipping techniques. Two master strokes were bringing in George McNeil and later Bert Logan as sprint and fitness coaches respectively. Neither, as I recollect, took a penny for their time but there were perks. Sitting at the front of the team bus was one and always being welcome in directors' boxes another. This arrangement suited both men as they were self-employed; it also suited the Hearts board, who didn't exactly throw money around.

The players' wage structure was such that success was rewarded by large bonuses to compensate for the low basic pay – to make for 'hungry fighters', perhaps. Remember the old chestnut:

'How do you spell bonus?'

'B-o-n-f-u-s'.

'But there's no F in bonus.'

'You got it!'

Sandy once told me what marked out the players who achieved greatness; to him, speed was the decisive factor. At the highest level, I would agree that this is true.

I have some experience of runners and running and know that a 'turn of foot' is an innate quality which can be found in runners who are not necessarily sprinters – a late surge by an 800m runner can destroy his or her rivals. 'The first five yards are in your head' is a well used expression in football and 'speed of anticipation' definitely makes for an advantage. The Celtic teams of the early '80s did not contain 'even time' sprinters but the ball was moved quickly, giving the impression of pace.

George Cowie, a full back, had joined the club from West Ham, where he had been offered a new contract. Instead he decided to throw in his lot with the Jam Tarts as he was sure that he could be a first team regular. Another stroke of genius was the signing of Jimmy Bone, who had returned from a spell in Hong Kong. Approaching the veteran stage of his career, this clever player was to be the perfect partner for the blossoming John Robertson. He was to benefit, too, from the management's skill in handling older players.

'Putting it all in' during the 90 minutes of a match was all that mattered. The older guys knew the game and responded to this sympathetic care. Donald Park, a former Tynecastle striker, returned from a spell with Partick. Something of 'a lad o' pairts', Donald is of diminutive but stocky build. He hails from Lochaber and whenever I see a Highland bull I think of him. Someone somewhere had told me that if you are small you've got to be better than those around you; and Alex MacDonald, Tommy McLean, Gordon Strachan and Parkie were all good, if not exceptional, in their time and the number of centre halves who have been pestered, irritated and frustrated by Donald is many.

Season 83–84 was anticipated with some excitement by the faithful in Gorgie. However Alex Ferguson, at that time the successful manager of Aberdeen, was of the opinion that the old legs in the Hearts team would be exhausted over the course of the season and relegation was guaranteed. Hearts went to Nairn to get some peace, quality training and three competitive matches. After a defeat by Inverness Caley, Henry Smith became firmly established as the No. 1 between the sticks, a development which John Brough, the previous incumbent, took well. Nairn County were no match for Hearts but Elgin proved to be stuffy, eventually going down to a fine strike by Cowie.

Closer to home, during a League Cup tie at Paisley, Walter Kidd was struck in the face by the ball. It was a freak incident and probably stung at the time but it appeared to be nothing to worry about. The next morning, 72 hours from the first meaningful derby match in years, I received a phone call from Walter. He told me that he had woken up that morning to find that he was blind in one eye. Well, you can imagine the alarm bells going off in my head. I had not been at the match but there had been no report of serious injury.

Due to the impact of the ball, blood had leaked into the front chamber of the eye, occluding the lens. All this I found out later from the Eye Pavilion staff. The remedy was, more or less, to lie down in a darkened room for 48 hours. Any exertion which might have raised Walter's blood pressure was strictly forbidden. He duly made a complete recovery but missed the eagerly awaited derby.

For Hearts, 'no more relegation' was the mantra. The season couldn't have got off to a better start, with five league wins out of five, including victories over Hibernian and Rangers. With two points for a win, the 10 points gained had almost banished relegation for that season. Next, in October 1983, a fine draw against Celtic was achieved at Parkhead, Bone's beautifully judged lob earning a point.

A Hearts Select in the author's home town of Lockerbie in 1983 for a friendly match with Mid-Annandale AFC. The Hearts players (in the dark jerseys). Back row: Callum McWright, Malcolm Murray, John Brough, Ian Westwater, Paul Cherry. Front row: Walter Borthwick (coach), Colin Plenderleith, Peter Marinello, Jimmy Sandison, Paddy Neilson, Gary Sutherland and Neil Irvine.

When a 2-0 defeat did come at home against a fine Aberdeen side, I was walking up the tunnel behind the manager after the final whistle when a fan leaned over and shouted at Alex: 'Is that the balloon burst?' Not being used to this ungrateful behaviour, I was about to give him a piece of my mind when Sandy grabbed my arm and led me away as if to say: 'That's show business.' How right he was.

As the season progressed, a sea change was taking place behind the scenes. A liaison was developing between the fans and the board and this gradually led to a reduction in crowd violence. The fences and barriers remained but Tynecastle was becoming a more welcoming ground for *all* the family. Hearts' excellent start in the league meant a healthy fifth finishing position.

In those early years with Hearts, I attended as many reserve matches and 'friendlies' as possible in order to learn as much as I could about all of the players. After one defeat, I was present when a trialist broke into song in the showers and witnessed how, with very little ceremony, reserve team coach John Binnie put paid to his solo.

Treatments which had been traditionally meted out to players in the guise of rehabilitation sometimes had more kinship to snake oil than to physiologically based therapeutics. I therefore set about developing a fail-safe, step-by-step physiotherapy programme: the player would progress from one stage to the next while continuing to perform at the previous level. With a system like this, if a player 'broke down', I would be able to ascertain at which stage or 'step' the setback had occurred. For any rehab programme to succeed the player's mindset had to be positive.

The highlight of season 83–84 was that we were unbeaten by our city rivals. A tall, quick left full back, Brian Whittaker, had arrived along with left midfielder Kenny Black, the latter escaping from a relegated Motherwell. The fine old campaigner Jimmy Bone would be replaced that October by a redoubtable Sandy Clark, another foil for JR. Their toughness and resilience meant that I would not have my work cut out for me with this trio.

With Kenny in the team Hearts had two natural left-sided players and this gave the team some balance as both Willie Johnston and Alex MacDonald were also 'Kerry footed'. It meant a lot to me that I had been at Hampden in 1966 for a Scotland–England game, and had seen Willie send in a corner which Denis Law dispatched with his head into Gordon Banks' right-hand 'postage stamp'. What a moment that was! I would never have imagined that 18 years later I would be fortunate enough to see Willie equalise against Celtic with a free kick, a superb *right*-footed strike low into Peter Latchford's left-hand corner.

Hearts made a shaky start in the domestic league season 84–85, but the fans still had a foray into Europe to look forward to. We were drawn in the UEFA Cup against PSG – Paris Saint-Germain – and the game was to be played at the Parc des Princes on 19 September.

The team was billeted in Versailles at the Trianon Hotel where the management had seen us coming – they shoved the players on to the top floor where they wouldn't embarrass their more sensitive guests.

This was my first trip abroad with Hearts but I didn't have much time to explore the neighbourhood as I was busy taping, stretching and massaging. I did manage one visit to the Parc des Princes before the game and was impressed, until I had a closer look at the pitch. One of the goal areas had been returfed and the replacement sods were thin with no depth in them at all. It was obvious that this was a cosmetic job.

And the match itself? Well, it was a game but no 'match' in the true sense. Hearts opened confidently with Gary Mackay missing a half chance during the early midfield sparring. Then the home team was awarded a free kick just outside the box. It was a fine shot but was the right height for Henry to save. However as he pushed from left to right the turf gave way under his foot, leaving him floundering and the ball scraped the inside of the post. 1-0. After that it was all one way. The final result was 4-0 to PSG. Despite a 2-2 draw in the return leg, Hearts exited the contest.

However, a memory to cherish was the sight of Wallace Mercer and Douglas Park kicking a ball about the Parc des Princes, two overweight tycoons rolling over the lush turf. As the Scottish middle-weight John McCormack once observed about a wrestler who fancied himself as a boxer: 'The ambition of every clown is to play Hamlet.'

CHAPTER 2

Bad Day at Dens

DEVON LOCH, RIDDEN by Dick Francis, collapsed five lengths clear and 40 yards from the winning post in the 1956 Grand National. Doug Sanders missed a three-foot putt, losing him the 1970 Open. Liverpool, only requiring a single point to win the 1988–89 League Championship, fell to a last-minute goal from Arsenal. The loss of the Scottish First Division championship in 1965, when Hearts were beaten at Tynecastle, allowing their massive tally of 90 goals to be trumped by Kilmarnock's superior goal average.

For Hearts, season 85–86 ranks alongside those iconic last-gasp sporting collapses.

As semi-finals go, the Scottish Cup clash with Dundee United at Hampden Park was a good match. John Colquhoun scored – which was enough to see Hearts victorious – with a dipping shot over the opposition keeper, Billy Thomson. John performed this type of strike many times during his career at Tynecastle. During a home game I remember Billy McNeill, The Hoops manager, dismissing one of his scoring strikes as 'an arse winder', implying that it was luck.

Not so. When something as accomplished as this happens, luck it ain't: it's the culmination of years of conditioning allied to talent. I can't say now whether it was a volley, a half-volley or if the ball just 'sat up' nicely for him. What I do know is that when a forward of Colquhoun's class strikes the ball towards the goal, it should be a surprise to no one when it hits the back of the net.

The fixture list determined that the very next week United were to host the Jambos. Tannadice must have housed one of its biggest ever crowds for the match. Nobody knew what to expect. A hangover from the previous Saturday? Revenge for United, who were still in contention for the league? Hearts fans needn't have worried. Sandy Clark hustled Hegarty into a less than convincing headed clearance. Lurking with intent, JR struck as fine a shot as most of us will be lucky to see again – a left-foot delivery into the keeper's right-hand corner. Poor Thomson couldn't have thrown his bonnet at it. The final result was 3-0 to the JTS. The next two games saw the reality of the situation dawn on the players. They were in the home straight to winning the league. But my inner apprehension was that on some level these two matches with United had had a draining effect.

Moving fixtures around to suit media coverage was not yet commonplace, but as it happened Aberdeen's visit the following week was put back to the Sunday to satisfy the television companies. A convincing argument has since been made that this change broke the Hearts' rhythm. Having lost the previous October at Tynecastle, Alex Ferguson was not going to have any side of his beaten twice at a ground where his team normally enjoyed success. In the event, the match was drawn, a brave Colquhoun goal equalising a rather soft penalty awarded to Aberdeen.

In the penultimate game of the season, at home against Clydebank, Gary Mackay kept the fans' hearts beating with a net-bulging strike at the Gorgie Road end. The park was dry and the ball bobbled just before he hit it, which made the strike all the more remarkable. With a 1-0 victory over the Bankies, Hearts were poised to be champions. Even a draw against Dundee the following week would be enough.

An uninspired St Mirren went down to a rampant Celtic at Love Street. They were hammered 5-0. As an ex-Rangers player, having his Old Firm rivals win the championship on his patch must have come as a huge disappointment to the Buddies manager, Alex Miller.

Everyone involved in that final league match will have an opinion of what went wrong, what conspired against Hearts. It was asked, why was an Edinburgh referee put in charge of the Dundee versus Hearts match? And, for a game of this importance, shouldn't the Hearts team have stayed at a Dundee hotel the night prior to the game, rather than treating it as a normal away fixture and travelling on the day of match?

'The wheel's aff the barra.' Alan Rae (right) with Alex MacDonald after the final whistle at Dens in 1986. © Eric McCowat Sports Photo Archive.

Could Craig Levein, who had fallen prey to a nasty gastro-intestinal bug, have played if he had been pumped full of anti-emetic drugs? (I don't think so: as he hadn't eaten for 48 hours, the tank would have been empty and a game of this magnitude was no place for a drained player.)

Bill Crombie, the match referee, later remarked to me that he had felt the tension in the air as soon as he entered the dressing room to inspect the boots. He also said he'd got the impression that the players were huddled together for comfort. The latter strikes me as highly unlikely – most probably Alex MacDonald had simply assembled them that way for his match talk.

Any Hearts fan who witnessed what unfolded in Dundee is unlikely ever to forget. The traumatic events of that May afternoon remain etched on my mind and it was not for lack of bottle that Hearts fell at the final hurdle. Guys like Sandy Jardine, Roddy McDonald, Kenny Black, Sandy Clark and Walter Kidd don't lose their nerve. My own belief is that the team had peaked in the double-header against United; on top of which, the realisation that they were within touching distance

The dejected Hearts team quitting the pitch after defeat at Hampden in 1986. Alan Rae is third from left, at the rear. © Eric McCowat Sports Photo Archive.

of the securing the championship – for the first time in over a quarter of century – may have psyched out some of the less experienced players.

Titles are not lost on the last day, they are lost over the course of the season and it is worth remembering the indifferent start Hearts had made to this league campaign. Losses against St Mirren, Aberdeen and Motherwell in the first quarter of the season did not enhance the cause. At Motherwell's ground I remember fielding the ball at a throw-in and shouting as I slung it at Craig Levein: 'We're playing for money!' Anything to galvanise the team! But at that stage, nobody anticipated that Hearts would be a contender for the league title.

There followed an unbeaten sequence. When I looked at the fixture list at Christmas 1985, I remember thinking Dens would be a hard place to get something from on the final day of the season – if we were chasing the title. An away game on a sloping pitch against a Dundee side with some decent players would always be tricky.

Changing a winning side for the biggest match in 20-odd years was never going to happen unless circumstances were forced upon the management: 'if it ain't broke, don't fix it'. But Craig Levein's absence on the day was unavoidable. On the bench (there was no dugout at

Dens) my colleague Tom Logan – no doubt under instructions – was keeping in touch (using a phone the size of a Niddrie brick) with what was happening at Love Street. I was never convinced that this was a good idea. The whole focus of our attention should have been on Hearts winning at Dens.

At half time Brian Whittaker was substituted. Brian was an athlete who would hardly heat up in a game such was the efficiency of his body, but the sweat was pouring out of him although it was a cool day (I remember that on the bench we were all wearing coats). There was something very wrong with Brian. Similar symptoms were affecting Kenny Black, another man you would always want on your side when things got tough.

When the first goal went in, with seven minutes left, there was no way back. There was an inevitability about the second. Dundee 2, Hearts 0.

Sandy Clark, during the first half, had gone down under a challenge in the penalty box. He reckoned that a penalty should have been awarded and would have been, had he been Robbo or JC. Did he go down too easily? I thought the defender was on the wrong side but he got away with it. Football is littered with such marginal decisions. However it had been a professional performance by the Edinburgh whistler, irrespective of his loyalties.

All credit to Sandy Jardine for his consideration of the officials' safety: he asked Bill Crombie to blow for time as soon as he was close to the players' gate in order to allow the officials to leave the field before the inevitable pitch invasion.

The atmosphere in the dressing room at full-time was funereal. No one wanted to speak. The more senior players had just seen their chance of a championship medal disappear in seven minutes, while youngsters like Gary Mackay, who at least did not feel that this would be their only chance of winning the league, were also extremely dispirited. Jardine tried a few words of solace but 'the ba' was burst'. Sandy Clark, never a sentimentalist, was the first to pick himself up and head off to the showers. I followed him to commiserate but no words were adequate and I went off to tidy up the kit.

Roddy McDonald, who had stepped in for Levein, was singled out for praise by both Alex and Sandy – deservedly so, as his performance had been exemplary, though it was scant consolation on an afternoon those of a maroon persuasion would rather forget. To this day I still have a picture in my mind of Walter Kidd, a real, solid Hearts man, lying along the back seat of the bus trying to drink a bottle of beer with the tears streaming down his face.

The day ended with the police routing the team bus out of Dundee behind the long line of retreating Hearts supporters. It was a cortege as far as the stunned travelling fans were concerned. (The polar opposite, of course, was taking place at Love Street in Paisley, as David Hay's Celtic celebrated the most unlikely of league title victories.) On arrival back at Tynecastle I noticed that a ground staff laddie who was waiting for the coach – above and beyond the call of duty – was crying. I might add he was not from Edinburgh but from Hamilton. The next morning Bill Crombie was going out for the Sunday papers when he found his car covered in chip fat and 'Celtic Rule' written in the goo.

After the calamity at Dens Park, the final of the Scottish Cup was always going to be something of a B movie. The squad stayed in a hotel in West Kilbride which had seen better days. However there was the sea air and the chance for the team to recharge.

The final, Ferguson's last before he left for Manchester, was well attended. Before the kick-off, when the referee, Mr Alexander, came into the dressing room to inspect the boots, all the players had whistles around their necks. This might have had something to do with the fact that the Aberdeen captain, Willie Miller, had a reputation for trying to influence decisions.

I should say that Aberdeen were an excellent team, being largely the side which had won the European Cup-Winners' Cup in Gothenburg. The game was not long started when Aberdeen forward John Hewitt hit a left-foot shot from the edge of the box. Henry Smith was moving to his right, the ball beating him into the left-hand corner of net. Aberdeen then sat back, allowing Hearts to press but without creating any scoring opportunities. That set the tone for the rest of the first half. Hearts unravelled in the second half, losing two further goals.

After a few verbals at a throw-in, Walter Kidd bounced the ball off the back of Willie Miller's head. Frustration had prevailed, he had done what many fans would have loved to do, so the referee had no alternative but to send him up the tunnel. In the space of a week, Hearts had lost the league and the cup. The heroic effort had fallen short, the dream had died. It was back to 'auld claes and porridge'.

Significantly, this was the last season BGS (Before Graeme Souness). After the arrival of this outstanding player at Ibrox, Scottish football would be transformed by money and start attracting big hitters from England, ensuring that smaller clubs like Hearts, Aberdeen, Dundee United and Hibs would not win the Premier League championship in a long time. A quarter of a century later, this remains the case.

In the aftermath of the loss of the league, I went over everything again and again, questioning the effectiveness of my own role. Could I, as an ad hoc member of the staff, have done any more to have helped the team? Overnight stays in hotels were fairly common practice before big matches, so should I have put in my tuppence worth when the decision was made *not* to follow this routine? Could we have dragged Craig from his sick-bed that morning, pumped him full of 'diamorph' (still legit in 1986) and risked playing an ill man? The game at Dens Park was lost in the final minutes. Now, looking back with the benefit of another 20 or so years' further mileage as a clinician, with all the knowledge I have gleaned over that time, I would say that it is possible that the players, collectively, were under-hydrated. This would have affected their performance, both mentally and physically, in the last 15 minutes of the match. I suspect hydration may also have been a factor in two arguably comparable episodes, Liverpool failing against Arsenal at Anfield and Celtic losing the title at Motherwell's ground, where both teams succumbed in the final minutes.

In July 1986 Hearts were invited to a tournament on the Isle of Man, a place more renowned for fearless motorcyclists and tax exiles than footballers. The crossing was smooth, which was more than could be said for the bus trip to the port. The Lendal Foot road left everyone

John Robertson and Kenny Black as the implications of the Hampden defeat sink in.
© Eric McCowat Sports Photo Archive.

feeling queasy. Generations of players taking that route, which snakes along the coast to Stranraer, must have felt the same way – what an advantage it must be for the inhabitants of Stair Park!

On the ferry the management were given silver service. I can remember trying to cut the meat. The knives supplied were bending under the effort! It was like chewing your way through a saddle.

Douglas in the summer is similar to Blackpool and Morecambe and Wattie B summed it up perfectly: 'No class!' Our seafront hotel could have been out of a *Fawlty Towers* set, with our host a ringer for Basil. Guests were mostly young, old, or, depending on one's taste, those available. Meals were geared for children and geriatrics and the mid-day fare served after training was meagre by ordinary standards, leaving the players famished. In light of this, the lads were allowed to supplement their diet by grazing along the stalls and takeaways on the promenade. It was difficult to maintain their focus; young men bursting with testosterone are like foxhounds waiting for a whiff of their prey – and there were foxes aplenty.

Hearts played three games in the Isle of Man Festival Trophy – against Wigan Athletic, the Bohemians of Dublin and Stoke City

– a draw, a win and a defeat. But the Hearts management were so scunnered with the place that a ferry was booked a day earlier than scheduled for our return. It was an early start back to Heysham. Very early. We hadn't time to pack thoroughly and kit that had been used the previous day was thrown into polythene bags instead of the (pre-war) hampers we had brought – a decision which was to prove costly. In those days a lot of ships' waste went over the side. Our kit was in the wrong place at the wrong time and somewhere on the voyage home the poly bags containing it were mistaken for kitchen waste and there was a premature burial at sea.

John Binnie, the reserve team coach, had been left in charge of the youngsters while the first team squad was pre-seasoning on the Isle of Man. Renovations at Tynecastle were being accelerated to cater for the better-off punters. Working through all this turmoil, John must have thought a boiler suit was more appropriate than the track variety.

The Hearts board had started to embrace the need for corporate support and the chairman was in his element: he had raffled a house at a match and had successfully attracted some sponsors, but now the big hitters were looking for more than a pie and Bovril. Hamilton bus proprietor Douglas Park and Wallace Mercer made an odd couple – they sparked off one another, which was good for the club. However there was a caveat. As my grandmother, the astute wife of an Annandale farmer used to say, : 'Ye cannae hiv twae cloakin hens in the yin nest.' The Hearts boardroom could not have been called a comfort zone.

The day after our return, a match against Stenhousemuir had been organised for those who had missed out on the Isle of Man sojourn. The occasion still evokes vivid memories. A player had arrived from England by the name of Wayne Foster. His quality had been endorsed by Hearts midfielder Neil Berry, who had known him when they were at Bolton Wanderers together. The day was wet and windy but the new arrival was as good as anything on the park (I should temper this comment, as wing half Jimmy Sandison also played). John must have been suitably impressed by Wayne's two goals as, on the strength of his appraisal, Wayne was later signed. The plusses were Wayne's pace and that he could play wide or through the middle.

New faces were indeed appearing at Tynecastle. Two youngsters, Scott Crabbe and a lad from the heartland of rugby union, Gary Parker, made their first appearances at a match against Newtongrange Star at the old Victoria ground – a venue to test the nerve of any youngster. As I approached the minibus which was to take us to 'Nittin', I saw this apparition in the front seat wearing a white jacket. Who the **** is this? 007 or Fred Astaire? I mused. It was Parker, who was quickly informed that front seats were for the top brass and not for some uppity punk in an outfit straight out of *Grease*. As the bus was leaving, Crabbe piped up: 'Al, have ye packed the oil?' That is similar to asking a jockey if he's brought his whip, so needless to say I ignored the question with splendid indifference!

A visit from Dukla Prague in the UEFA Cup in September 1986 would be a test of Hearts' progress and I was pleased at my efforts with Neil Berry, who made an earlier than expected recovery from a hamstring tear, enabling him to be in the line-up for what proved to be a cracking tie.

Alex MacDonald once told me that European nights were special to him as a player. I can understand that. There is something theatrical about playing under the lights and, particularly if there is a little dampness on the pitch, the movement of the ball speeds up, making the players react more quickly.

Dukla played their part, scoring twice. Sandy Clark scored one, followed by Foster's contribution. As I recall, he chested a throw-in from his mate Berry and ran a few strides before blasting a right-footer high into the net at the Gorgie Road end. A photographer caught the immediate reaction from Wayne. A stunning picture of his youthful exuberance may still be hanging in the Tynecastle Arms. The winning goal, inevitably, came from JR.

In 1986 the Berlin Wall was still standing and the Czech Republic was part of Czechoslovakia. Everyone had heard of the Prague Spring, when the Czech people tested the patience of the old Soviet regime. A visit to Prague to play the army team, Dukla, was therefore greeted with mixed feelings.

Boarding the bus to play Dukla in Prague in the UEFA Cup, 1986.
Ian Jardine, Andy Watson, Alan Rae, Brian Whittaker and Andy Bruce.

The air controllers at Prague kept the Hearts charter flying round in circles for half an hour – an army team is not without influence. When we finally disembarked, the airport looked like the Carlisle equivalent on a Sunday – deserted. My wife Sheila and I had spent our honeymoon in the Soviet Union, so I had some idea of what to expect from Iron Curtain countries. Trip organiser Ian Dinwoodie had secured a central hotel for us. Vice chairman Pilmar Smith, the livewire Jimmy Caldwell and I rose early to walk to Wenceslas Square before training commenced. I was surprised how far Prague had gone to loosen its Communist bonds – there was no real shortage of essentials and some luxury items were available, although generally of local manufacture.

There is a paranoia which visits teams when playing abroad: what tricks or cheap shots are the opposition going to try? It had started for us with the flight into Prague. The next morning we set off for training in a minibus provided by Dukla. Did it break down? Of course it did.

The stadium was big and a lot less Stalinesque than some I had visited, and the pitch was satisfactory. The army influence could be seen in the way the dressing room was laid out with military precision.

But groundsmen are the same the world over and within minutes of our allocated time expiring, the familiar 'Get aff that park', or the Czech equivalent, rang out.

Dukla's coaches must have expected a similar Scottish approach to the second encounter. But our management team had other ideas. Although I don't have the professional insight of a coach, I could see we were going to sit back and absorb whatever the opposition came up with. This worked well and initially had Dukla nonplussed. In the second half the hosts were less cautious. They had read the first-half situation, came out attacking, and soon had Henry Smith picking the ball out of the back of the net. With the damage done Dukla retreated, knowing the tie was won on away goals, although their hearts must have skipped a beat after JR was upended in the box near the end. The referee, who had officiated at Tynecastle, waved away the claims for a penalty. Perhaps that was justice, considering how Sandy Clark had clattered the Dukla keeper, allowing Robbo to score the winner in the first leg. We were beaten but Hearts had given an improved performance against one of Eastern Europe's better sides.

A little light relief was provided on the way home in the form of a practical joke involving Jimmy Caldwell, a friend of the vice chairman, who had purchased some expensive Prague crystal. Refusing to have it stowed in the hold, he opted for the safer alternative of carry-on luggage, but on the flight to Heathrow his concentration wandered and his precious parcel of crystal was substituted with some empty miniatures and cheap glassware.

On our way to Customs after landing, a player snatched this precious cargo from Jimmy and proceeded to play touch rugby with it. The parcel was tossed around between players and eventually crashed onto the floor to the sound of breaking glass. Jimmy went ballistic. He grabbed a fire bucket and threw it over the guilty and the innocent. The penny only dropped when he was reunited with his purchases intact. Life was never dull with the Jam Tarts.

CHAPTER 3
Craig, the Fife Flyer

ONE OF THE MOST gifted players I had the honour of working with at Tynecastle was Craig Levein. Dressing room life was never dull with him around, whether he was throwing his tuppence worth into the ring during the manager's team talk or landing a right-hook worthy of Mike Tyson on the nose of a team-mate. Levein certainly made his mark in more ways than one but there is no doubt the club would have been a far worse place without him.

The statistics – more than 400 games for Hearts and 16 caps for his country – fail to tell the full story of this complex character who endured more than his fair share of injury misery while at Hearts.

It all started back in 1983, when a tall, dark-haired Fifer starred for Cowdenbeath against Hearts in the first leg of a League Cup tie at Central Park. Hearts scraped through on penalties after the home leg but all the talk among the directors was about the colossus at the heart of Cowden's defence, who became a priority signing for the Jam Tarts. To sign such a talent – for £40,000 – was a real coup for the management team, who, like Field Marshall Allenby on meeting T.E. Lawrence, had known a good thing when they saw it. Craig, who was SFPA Young Player of the Year in *both* 1985 and 1986, was tall, athletic and seriously quick. As a top player at Hibernian, Dundee United and Hearts, Darren Jackson, put it: 'It didn't matter how much space or time you thought you had against Craig – you hadn't any!' To say that Craig had 'a bit about him' would be to undersell him.

Even at 19, he had more than a little insight about life in general. There was the rub – managers do not often invite comments from their playing staff, especially during the half time break, when the atmosphere can be explosive. Craig was not one to take criticism without a riposte and this could cause a serious ignition. At his work in an electronics factory, he would have been exposed to the rough and tumble of the shop floor, where foremen or chargehands expected to get a bit of come and go from the staff. Like most of us he knew what it meant to cope with low wages – something today's pampered players going into the game straight from school might benefit from.

In my 23 years at Hearts I worked with eight managers. As manager from 2001 to 2005, Craig was one of the three most successful, the other two being Alex MacDonald and Jim Jefferies, two men who also knew about life on the 'outside' – as cooper and insurance rep, respectively. Levein's playing career was cut short in painful and frustrating circumstances. I see his success on the other side of the touchline as being a refocusing of his obsessive desire to scale the heights in the world of soccer.

At the end of October 1986, following a suspension, it was decided to play Craig in a reserve match against Hibernian at Easter Road. Tom Logan was watching from the sidelines as he went up for a header and twisted his knee on landing. The effect of this innocuous looking incident was devastating.

Reconstructive surgery of the knee joint is now commonplace, fibre optics and micro-surgical instruments allowing surgeons to repair the internal structures of the joint with the minimum of trauma. When I started as a junior physiotherapist, a torn cartilage would be completely removed and the patient hospitalised for 7 to 10 days; if an infection developed, recovery might take months. A ruptured cruciate ligament could be diagnosed clinically by observation of symptoms and handling of the joint – but there was no surgical remedy on offer. Adapt, adjust, or quit were the options.

By the mid-1980s a torn ligament might be replaced with a Dacron artificial ligament, which looks rather like a pyjama cord. After it has been surgically inserted and anchored to the two bones of the knee joint, natural body materials infiltrate the loosely woven mesh, which acts as a scaffold, producing an almost natural replacement in 6 to 18 months. A Dacron ligament was used on Craig's knee. Over the

Craig Levein (left), Alex MacDonald and John Robertson.
© Eric McCowat Sports Photo Archive.

next nine years, that knee and its owner would never be far from my thoughts. As soon as he came out of hospital I became closely involved in his rehabilitation. He followed the long rehab process to the letter. Youth was on his side. He was under 25, the cut-off point between youth and the slow decline we are all fated to enjoy. To support the sort of surgery he had undergone it is vital that muscles are strengthened gradually. This experience would prove invaluable when I was involved in guiding the several other unfortunate Hearts players who later sustained this injury.

Almost a year to the day of his injury Craig made his return, playing most of a match against Rangers at Ibrox. After a wee jolt it was decided to bring him off. Learning to function with an artificial ligament inside the knee was taking time. The part of the brain which controls movement is dependent on incoming information from joints, tendons, ligaments and muscles, in a process called proprioception. There was obviously an area which was failing to relay this postural information to Craig's 'Head Office'. The prime suspect had to be the Dacron ligament. However, it functioned well in the matches that followed until, on 16 January 1988, Graeme Souness and Rangers rode into town to play a league match. Mark Walters, a fine English left winger, challenged Craig on the touchline at the Gorgie Road end, in front of the standing enclosure. A lesser player might have put the ball into row Z but Craig opted for a ball up the line. After the delivery the knee twisted awkwardly as it made contact with the ground. The ligament had failed. It had lasted for 21 first team games.

I doubt if there was anyone present in the crowd who did not feel for young Craig as he was taken from the field. Everyone associated with Hearts was devastated, from the chairman to tea ladies Ella and Mary. The physical aspect of injury is often easier to deal with than the psychological and social impacts. My heart went out to Carol, Craig's wife, who had sustained her husband during the long days of doubt and uncertainty. Incidentally, we now know that there had been some covert interest in Craig from Rangers – and so that possibility had also been shattered.

The physicality and speed of the game was leading to an increase in cruciate damage among players but reconstructive knee surgery had evolved since Craig's original injury. Dacron did not allow an early return to sporting activity and by now artificial fibres had been overtaken by donor tissue and there were no rejection problems with strips of natural tendon taken from a donor site in the same body, usually from the same limb. This was the next procedure Craig was put through. It stalled his career progression for another year and Hearts lost the central rock of their defence.

We found out during this second period of rehab just how special Craig was. A machine had been developed (the Cybex) on which muscles could be tested objectively – full recovery was not a matter of opinion any more. Tested on this kit, Craig's injured knee showed more speed and strength than any others examined, apart from rugby internationalist John Rutherford. These two supreme athletes both showed phenomenal recuperative powers, superior to the others tested, none of whom had undergone two previous major operations.

On 21 January 1989, wearing the number six jersey, Craig returned to the first team for an away game against Dundee United. Naturally I was on edge but no more so than the big fellow himself. This game was going to be the acid test. Reserve matches are good preparation but no substitute for a match with points and money riding on the result.

Before a recent Wales versus England rugby union international, I had put an elasticated support on the referee to help him through (he had sustained a hamstring injury). I had watched the game closely on TV and was satisfied that the orthosis was practically invisible. A similar type was acquired for Craig for the Dundee match. In addition I covered it with face cream, for further camouflage. To our delight – not to mention relief – the knee came through with flying colours.

Minor injuries often plague players who are returning to the first team after a long absence. The next week was a home cup-tie against Ayr United. Craig managed to 'turn' his ankle a few days before this match. He was desperate to play and we resorted to measures which would never be taken today to ensure his participation. A local injection was given by Dr Melvin and a strapping applied which was reinforced by a canvas ankle brace with aluminium stays. How did Craig walk, never mind play? Hearts won the match in front of a decent crowd, some of whom I suspect came primarily to witness Craig's comeback. The following season the second operation proved its worth. Craig played over 40 games. Tendon transplants were the way forward and would save the careers of thousands of sports people, amateur and professional.

Season 89–90 saw the Hearts team return to free-scoring form. A cup-tie in Aberdeen at Pittodrie which was lost 4-1 in a second-half onslaught by the home side was, I think, the beginning of the end for Alex MacDonald's management.

After three defeats at the start of the next season from Premier opposition, Dunfermline, Aberdeen and Rangers, Alex MacDonald was sacked. Wattie B. and John Binnie left with him. Otis Spann had been singing about a 'Sad Day In Texas'. Well, it was a sad day in Gorgie.

It was a stressful time and when the human body comes under

stress, it will find an outlet. Everyone is different in this respect and in Craig's case it was his neck which plagued him. Before a derby match at Easter Road he was having a typical episode but it didn't stop him from scoring with his head at the Dunbar End, past a rooted Andy Goram. Everyone was delighted, including Hearts left back Tosh McKinlay, who, in celebration, wrapped his arm around Craig's neck in a wrestler's lock!

A story about this piece of anatomy comes from Craig himself. While suffering one episode of neck pain, he set off to see a therapist in the Perth area, his wife driving and Craig lying in the passenger's seat with the back down to relieve his tortured upper spine. To an outside observer it would have appeared that Carol was alone in the car. During the journey a macho male driver forced her to stop on a slipway. He had just got out of his car to give her some verbals when the passenger's seat slowly rose to reveal a rather testy husband. In the fracas that followed, Macho Man no doubt wished his underwear had been of the disposable variety.

Amidst all the fun and games, Craig was selected for Scotland's World Cup squad in Italia '90, a truly remarkable achievement after undergoing extensive pioneering knee surgery and a credit to him and his home team.

After the Dnepr match in the Ukraine in 1990, Joe Jordan was appointed manager at Hearts. Jordan's playing reputation was peerless. I was later to meet his primary school teacher, who described him as reserved, obedient, tidy and respectful. The child was the father of the man. At his first meeting in the players' lounge, the Hearts young centre half Alan McLaren got to know the score when he addressed the new manager as Joe. There was a pause. 'It's Boss, Alan.' And so it was to be.

While Craig and Mr Jordan did not always get on, the new manager's attention to detail and his tactical awareness rubbed off on Craig. Joe had played previously with AC Milan and what AC didn't know about the game wasn't worth knowing. At Hearts he made sure that hours were spent on the 'shape' of the team, placing emphasis on every player knowing how to play their position in a match. Jordan was manager until May 1993, when a catastrophic result at Falkirk (6-0) brought his era to an end. Sandy Clark, the popular Jambo centre forward, was then appointed manager with Hugh McCann as his assistant.

Hearts were soon embarking on a European adventure, having qualified for the UEFA Cup almost by default; the break-up of the old Yugoslavia possibly had something to do with the club's admission to the tournament, as they had only achieved fifth position in the SPL the previous season.

A home tie against Atlético Madrid ended with Hearts taking a narrow lead to the Spanish capital. The return leg was an untidy affair and a painful experience for Craig. He suffered a broken cheek bone after Henry Smith felled him in the box as they both rose to clear the ball. This latest injury would keep the big centre half out for a month. What was it about Hearts and broken cheek bones? Dave Bowman, Gary Mackay (two) and now Craig.

At this time, the sale of the club to Chris Robinson and Leslie Deans – another change of management, with all the upheaval that involves – had everyone apprehensive about the future, including myself. 'A new broom sweeps clean', as they say. Sandy Clark and Hugh McCann, their efforts to keep Hearts in the Premier League largely ignored, were dismissed.

The two Toms, McLean and Forsyth, then arrived. An uneventful pre-season got under way and, as with any new management team, new ideas and new formations were tested. Nothing, though, could have prepared manager Tommy McLean for the scene which was to unfold during a friendly with near neighbours Raith Rovers at Stark's Park.

Hearts had three central defenders on the park: Craig Levein, Alan McLaren and Graeme Hogg. Two goals down approaching half time, the game was not going according to plan and the mood in the camp was far from cheery. At one stage Alan had said to Graeme, 'Hoggie, we are playing in maroon!' A normally docile lad with his own brand of humour, Graeme must have felt insulted. After all, hadn't he played 60 consecutive games for Manchester United? Hadn't he told the lads in the dressing room that when they were standing outside Old Trafford looking for tickets he was inside marking Maradona?

Worse was to follow. As referee Bill Crombie prepared to blow for half time I bent down to grab the pitch bag and when I looked up there was a Hearts player horizontal on the edge of his own box. Play was over, so there was no need to wait for a summons from the ref. What a sight greeted me as I raced onto the field, somewhat puzzled, to assess the situation. Graeme was down and there was blood everywhere. He wasn't going to make the count.

While I summoned a stretcher, Bill Crombie ran over with a red card (not for me as it was the interval). 'And I'm giving you one as well!' he declared, looking at the prostrate player and flourishing the card above his head. What on earth was going on here? My first duty was to attend to Hoggie and so I set about reviving him. He was carried into the medical room beneath the grandstand, where the Raith doctor could inspect the damage. I left them to it.

I headed for the dressing room, still with no idea what had happened. Had a Rovers player been sent off? There had indeed been another dismissal. One glance in Craig's direction, and the grim reality hit home. His head was in his hands. The manager was pacing the floor, utterly speechless. Did someone say a 'friendly'? 'Welcome to the Hearts, Tommy,' I said.

Apparently Graeme had made a lunge at Craig. As already mentioned, Craig had astonishingly quick muscles and after years of refinement through hitting the speed ball during rehab, you can imagine the speed and power of the blow which floored Graeme and broke his nose. Craig was a handy boy.

We might have thought the damage had been done but worse was to follow. Some sad freak in the crowd had filmed the scene and was to make a fast buck by selling the evidence to the media. Eventually the authorities acted, banning both players for 10 games. This episode effectively ended Graeme's stay at Tynecastle. A pity, as he had a sweet left foot and a great leap, the latter benefiting from huge calf muscles. But he wasn't a fighting man.

With Graeme on his way, a very under-rated centre half was signed.

Craig Levein, Jambo trade unionist Alec Kitson and master builder James Clydesdale, in 1995 after the demolition of the School End terracing.

Willie Jamieson, a former Hibernian favourite, a centre forward converted to centre back, would help to fill the gap and partner Davie McPherson, who had returned from Rangers for a second time.

This season would be a white-knuckle ride for the spectators. In spite of the lengthy ban, Craig played for three-quarters of the season. There were two wins and two draws against Celtic, which went a long way to keeping Hearts in the top flight. The Hearts' old guard had done their best in a turbulent campaign.

The two Toms left in the summer of 1995, after reducing the wage bill. Enter a former captain of Hearts, Jim Jefferies, as manager. Once again a new regime and new ideas. The partnership of Jefferies and Billy Brown was going to have its work cut out as an ageing squad increasingly threw more weight on the defenders, and it wasn't long before Craig sustained another injury to his troublesome knee.

The venue was Tynecastle, the occasion a League Cup tie against Dunfermline on 30 September 1995. One of the Pars players overran the ball and Craig nipped in to take the ball away under control. How he must have wished he had cleared it differently. His career might have been saved, at least temporarily, if he had booted it into row Z.

But then, that wasn't the style of this cultured centre half.

There was a clash of legs and Craig had to leave the field. Neil Berry, who came on as sub, was also clattered and had to leave the field for stitches. I don't think any of us, including Craig, knew that his playing career had ended. Attrition had finally taken its toll; wear and tear from the many games he had played, often against the odds, had destroyed the joint. Further procedures were performed to shore it up before it became absolutely clear that this was the end game. Both of us were affected by this dawning realisation. Finally an emotional press conference was held and Craig announced his retirement. He had enjoyed between eight and nine good years, a lamentably short career for such an exceptional player.

To a lesser person the wilderness might have beckoned, but instead it was Cowdenbeath. For Craig this was the first rung on the managerial ladder and an ascent which led to his appointment as manager of the Scotland national team.

A memory which has stuck with me is the silhouette of Carol and Craig walking down the tunnel into the sun with their daughter Christie, to wave to the fans attending his testimonial match. It put me

Vale do Lobo mid-season 2002–03 group photo showing eight of Levein's signings. Back row: Craig Levein (manager), Steven Boyack, Jean Louis Valois, Phil Stamp, Kevin McKenna, Robbie Neilson, Gary Wales, Craig Gordon, Mark De Vries, Andy Webster, Scott Severin, Andy Kirk, Neil Janczyk, John Harvey (kit manager), Neil MacFarlane, Peter Latchford (goalkeeping coach), Steven Pressley. Front row: Stéphane Mahé, Peter Houston (assistant manager), Austin McCann, Alan Maybury, Stephen Simmons, Joe Hamill, Graham Weir.

in mind of an iconic image from John Wayne's best film, *The Searchers*, when at the end, with his mission accomplished, he walks out of the ranch-house door, silhouetted against the sun, to an uncertain future.

In 2000 Jefferies and Brown left, the latter, it has to be said, having been sacked without due acknowledgement of the extent of his contribution. The speed with which the board acted reminded me of how surgeons amputate quickly to reduce the shock.

The next appointment to the manager's job was a no-brainer. After all, the candidate was looking after a sideshow to stock car racing in Cowdenbeath FC, aka 'The Blue Brazil'! Craig duly arrived with Jefferies' previous coach, Peter Houston, who resisted the lure of Bradford City, where the Jefferies' management had gone. The pair were understandably excited at the prospect of working at Hearts' new academy, based at Heriot-Watt University, which Chris Robinson had set up.

Craig, nothing if not his own man, left his players in no doubt as to what was expected after a poor result against Aberdeen at Pittodrie. Holidays that coincided with the winter league shutdown were cancelled – it would have been a treat to watch the WAGS' faces when that piece of news was brought home! The pre-booking of the annual mid-season trip to Vale do Lobo was also knocked on the head after a disastrous result against Falkirk in the Scottish Cup. A line in the sand had been drawn and those on the wrong side wouldn't be around for long.

An incident I can look back on now with a smile, but which at the time was no laughing matter, was Craig's altercation with a magnetic tactics board. It was half time in a home match and he took a massive swipe at the board – to impress the players, no doubt – but only succeeded in breaking his fifth metacarpal!

'Maverick', 'non-conformist', 'off the wall' – all are terms that come to mind when one examines Craig's signings. 'Under-achievers', 'second-raters', 'in and outers' are a few more. But the guys in question could never be described as being bland, particularly former Celtic star Stéphane Mahé, who when at Parkhead, turned up with a Mohican-style haircut dyed green!

An interesting arrival in season 2001–02 was Jamaican player Ricardo Fuller. He came to Hearts on loan from Crystal Palace, where he had been quite recently signed. His performance had been affected by a knee problem and he been on a break in Jamaica before coming to Edinburgh with his mother in tow (not surprisingly, as many of the Caribbean islands are matriarchal societies).

A product of Jamaica's youth academy, Ricardo had been played and trained to impress, often when he was going through a growth phase. He was just one of the huge number of kids in football who suffer growth-related problems. With rest and a period away from the game, the majority recover but the less fortunate end up under a surgeon's knife. Two youngsters at Hearts in the early '80s required spinal surgery. Thankfully both recovered well – one was eventually capped for Scotland – but the condition should not have been allowed to become so disabling. To this day far too many youngsters, victims of over zealous parents and crackpot coaches, develop serious lower back problems.

I don't think Ricardo took to Scotland but there's no doubt he had talent. The trouble was that there needed to be two balls on the park, one for him and one for the other 21 players. When he was in the mood he was unstoppable, he had more tricks than a bag of ferrets, but he required the stern discipline which comes with professionalism. His stay in Gorgie marked a turning point for him. What he learned with the Jambos prepared him for better things down south, where he was the subject of several decent moves.

I always smile when I think how Wilfred Ouiefio, one of Craig's less inspired signings, inspired me to my best ever snowman impersonation (not that I make a habit of it). A right-sided midfielder, he was picked for a first team game against Motherwell soon after his arrival in 2002, but as it turned out he lacked the physical presence to make an impact in the SPL and wasn't around for long.

Wilfred was one of the many players I worked with for whom English was not their first language. As far as I am concerned, it is incumbent on the staff to make an attempt at being understood –

accents from Tranent, Wallyford, Newtongrange and Musselburgh are fine if you are a local. In the physio's room I had a selection of music I played from time to time, sometimes to the players' displeasure – Paul Ritchie gave me pelters about it when interviewed by a tabloid reporter – but it could help foreigners to get a hold on words and phrases. One day while Wilfred was undergoing treatment I let him have Desmond Dekker, full blast. He liked it so much that when I offered the disc to him he nearly broke my wrist.

Depending on who the manager was at the time, the backroom staff had a Christmas night out. Nothing outrageous, just some pasta and a few beers. On one such occasion we were just sitting down to our meal when my phone rang. It was George Wright, his agent, calling from his mother's guest house, where Wilfred was billeted. 'There's something far wrong with Wilfred's foot, he can't come down the stairs and he's in agony!' he exclaimed.

Leaving the rest of the staff to tuck into their dinner, I met George at A&E in the old Royal Infirmary. Wilfred was eventually stretchered into a cubicle and he lay there for a couple of hours with a raging fever and several lumps the size of hazelnuts in his groin until being transferred to the Infectious Diseases Unit at the Western General, where antibiotics were to be administered intravenously. Wilfred was feeling pretty sick and gey far fae hame. It had also put the kibosh on my Christmas night out! But this was not a case of 'out of sight, out of mind'. It troubled me when I thought of the youngster lying in hospital, in a ward surrounded by strangers, treated by foreign doctors and being served exotic Scottish food.

Not many people know this, but there was a quotation from St Matthew's gospel above the front door of the old Edinburgh Royal Infirmary which went: 'I was sick and ye visited me, I was a stranger and ye took me in.' When I was first employed there, I found this quote memorable and maybe it made me think more of Wilfred's plight. It was Christmas Eve and the snow started in the afternoon. By three o'clock it was thick *and* lying. Taking a car across the hill to the Western General would be tricky but I thought I would be able to leg it there and back in about an hour.

The staff in the Hearts shop gave me a massive bar of chocolate for the lad, so with this in hand and humming 'Good King Wenceslas', I set off. With the snow causing all sorts traffic problems, walking was a smart but tiring choice. The nursing staff on his ward took pity on this partial snowman and pointed out Wilfred's bed to me. The screens were drawn, which made me think he'd either popped his clogs or was on a bed pan. I called his name. After a moment or two the screens parted slightly, just enough for this gorgeous blonde head to appear. Well, I was speechless. 'Wilfred's fine,' she said huskily, as blondes do, 'would you like to see him?' Not for me to be the gooseberry, I lobbed in the chocolate, wished him a 'joyeux Noel' and left feeling more than slightly bemused. Not everyone gets that kind of therapy when hospitalised!

Returning to Craig Levein, my most singular memory is perhaps the return leg against Portuguese side Braga, after he had successfully guided Hearts into the group stages of the UEFA Cup. I embraced him after the match, saying, 'You're a millionaire now!' Hearts were now in a league section of a European trophy. His big centre forward De Vries had done the business. Both reputations were enhanced.

Fate dictated that he never had the time to enjoy Hearts' European adventure to its maximum, the lure of England and Leicester City proving too strong for this ambitious individual. His departure took me by surprise as I honestly thought he was in it for the long haul at Tynecastle. It left me a little saddened as we had experienced many special moments together.

Under Craig, chances were taken in the transfer market and the players coming to Hearts either looked on their move as a step up or a step down. Both attitudes tested his man-management skills but, as he has proved since his days in the Gorgie hot seat, there are few better equipped in that department. When he eventually left for Leicester City he had gained valuable experience with a famous Scottish club, buying, selling, coaching and inspiring a host of players whose careers were enhanced by working under him at Hearts.

CHAPTER 4

High Road to Munich

IN THE CLOSE SEASON before 88–89, a gap was left in the Jambos' strike force as John Robertson had taken flight to become a Magpie at St James' Park. Robbo was a firm favourite with the supporters. He was two-footed, scored prolifically and he was on the short side. As we all know, Scottish football supporters love wee guys, particularly when they can play a bit. (My predecessor, Andy Stevenson, nicknamed him 'Tweakie' – after John 'tweaked his back'.)

'The Chairy', Wallace Mercer, desperate to keep the fans on-side, signed Dundee United's Iain Ferguson. I had seen this striker in action and will never forget one occasion at Tannadice when he punished the Jambos with a fine, lofted shot from 45 yards, which dipped under Henry Smith's crossbar. After Iain completed the paperwork I was given the task of escorting him to the Hearts training camp in Germany. During the flight I was quite taken aback when a diffident Iain spoke of Robbo's qualities. He wasn't as good as JR, he said, and was concerned that the fans would expect too much of him as the replacement for a wee local hero. I did my best to reassure him, mentioning that Hearts was really a family club and once he knocked in a goal or two his worries on that score would disappear.

Alex MacDonald's third campaign in European competitions began with an away tie against the Dublin side, St Patrick's. Without Robbo the responsibility for scoring goals would be spread over the likes of Foster, Galloway, Colquhoun, Ferguson and Bannon. The first leg was a towsy affair, which was not unexpected since the tie involved two teams from the Celtic Fringe. Towards the end Henry Smith had to be carried off after a tackle left him with three-inch gouge in his shin. Hearts ran out as 2-0 winners. The return leg at Tynecastle was a more subdued affair. Again it was a 2-0 win for the home side; 4-0 on aggregate.

A glamour tie in the next round would have pleased everybody. What the Jambos got was the chance to play in Vienna, football of course. The first leg against Austria Vienna was to be played at Tynecastle. A non-scoring draw at home can often be better than a result where the opposition get on the score sheet, as away goals can double up in the event of a draw in the second leg. The harshness of professional soccer was demonstrated when, before the second leg, Sandy Jardine was sacked from his post as co-manager. This was a poignant moment for me. Sandy had introduced me to the club and was a great help to me as a clinician who at times struggled to understand the intricacies of the professional game.

In Vienna my time was taken up with Walter Kidd's foot injury which had been sustained the previous Saturday. All sorts of taping combinations were tried before a formula was found which would keep Walter in the team. On a frosty night at the Prater Stadium, in the second half, Walter received a pass from Eamonn Bannon, took off down the line and crossed the ball for Iron Mike to finish with a header at the near post. Now Vienna needed to score twice, which they didn't do. Herbert Prohaska, a famous Austrian international player, was on the park that night, but he should have stayed at home as he was totally outplayed by Jimmy Sandison. Hearts achieved a fine victory but were to lose Wayne Foster for two months from an ankle injury received in the early minutes of the first half.

As autumn edged into winter Hearts had, for once, the chance of progressing beyond the New Year in a European competition, if they could survive the next round. The turmoil in the former Yugoslavia was going to figure in the minds of players and staff at Tynecastle when Velež Mostar came to visit. A good home result was essential in order to survive what was likely to be a hostile second leg in the Balkans. The scoring load had been spread successfully in earlier rounds and Galloway's worth was beginning to show. In the home leg Bannon, Galloway and Colquhoun looked to have made the tie safe, once

Heart of Midlothian chairman Wallace Mercer, Craig Levein, John Robertson and manager
Alex MacDonald. © Eric McCowat Sports Photo Archive.

again the away side had failed to score – a big plus for the next leg.
As it happened, I couldn't travel to Mostar. So my colleague Malcolm
Colquhoun stood in for me. It was going to be a harrowing experience
for the young physiotherapist. There was plenty of intimidation from
the local population at the hotel and the stadium but Hearts kept their
collective nerve by scoring a vital away goal, a header from Mike,
which put the tie to bed.

Three rounds, six matches, two goals conceded. Remaining teams
in the competition would take notice of the Gorgie boys and perhaps
not relish a visit to Edinburgh.

The prospect of Hearts playing one of the finest sides in Europe had
Jambos of all ages desperate to attend a fixture which was going to be
an all ticket affair. I can say without contradiction that Bayern Munich,
the team which had won three consecutive European championships,
matched a previous visit to Tynecastle by International Milan in 1960.
Today it is unlikely that a tie like this would be possible due to the
seeding system devised to protect the powerful sides from exiting the
competition in an early round. I suspect that television companies

have had some influence here. Hearts had nothing to fear playing 'on their own midden'. Having seen off the sides from Dublin, Vienna and Mostar in the autumn, confidence was high. This would be Alex MacDonald's 11th European tie while he was supremo at Tynecastle. Added to these experiences were his performances with Rangers as a player when they competed annually in international competitions.

Tynecastle in the depths of winter was a dreary place. By this time of the season the pitch was well worn, the track surrounding frozen hard into ruts, and then there was ' the shed', a dark, satanic structure which housed a mean corps of diehards. Surrounding all the standing areas was a 12-foot wire mesh fence.

Bayern sent their team bus ahead of the team on a ferry while the players and officials flew into Edinburgh so that it could convey them directly to their hotel without any delay. I wonder if, on passing Murrayfield, they thought it was the venue for the match. If so, a shock was in store.

Newcastle United had recently sacked their manager, Liam McFaul. This paved the way for John Robertson to return after a short stay at St James' Park. Alex MacDonald, however, preferred to stick with the blond, blue-eyed Iain Ferguson as the main striker on the night of the match. With his looks and ability, he would not have been out of place in the away ranks. This selection was to prove decisive. A player who had come through the youth system at Tynecastle was to make his European debut; this was Alan McLaren, an 18-year-old full back. He was to play his part in what was to be a memorable night in Gorgie.

During the first half of the game, what had been considered as a little off-shore problem by the Bavarians was becoming more uncomfortable for them by the minute. This discomfort was reinforced at half time when they trooped off into the cramped dressing room, where hospitality consisted of sweet, milky tea served out of an old aluminium kettle.

About ten minutes into the second half, the Jam Tarts were awarded a free kick outside the left-hand side of the box. Having attended Kenny Black, who had been the victim of the foul, I retreated from the field of play. As the free kick was about to be taken I crouched behind

Raimond Aumann's goal to avoid blocking the view of the crowd. Tosh McKinlay 'touched' the ball into the path of Fergie, who struck it perfectly. It whizzed past Aumann into the right-hand corner of the net. This was technique of the highest quality and accuracy.

At 1-0, the next 30 minutes became stressful for non-playing staff and supporters alike. On the pitch the Hearts boys were just enjoying themselves and the score remained the same at full time. Everybody had a thoroughly good time, save the Germans, who probably felt relieved at losing only one goal on, for them, an evening best forgotten.

CHAPTER 5
New Faces

AT THE END of season 89–90 Hearts were invited to an international youth tournament in the northern French town of Croix. In the touring party were up and coming Tom Harrison, Micky Watters, Max Christie, Andy Paterson and a goalkeeper who eventually played for the senior team, Gary O'Connor. Also in the party was a trialist who I will call Tony Solari. Carrying the biggest hold-all I had ever laid eyes on, he was obviously something of a dandy, but he would soon come crashing back down to earth.

There was a quartet of 'technical staff': Walter Borthwick, first team coach at Tynecastle; Sandy Clark, youth team coach; Peter McCloy, goal keeping coach; and myself.

Excited at the prospect of our little adventure, we flew out to Bruxelles from Newcastle in a plane that was only slightly bigger than the bus we had just disembarked from. We were accommodated in a school gymnasium which was divided to house a Dutch outfit and ourselves. Walter and Peter got the hotel, Sandy and I drew the short straw and were in with the boys. I was grateful for Sandy's presence as he sorted out any nonsense coming from the unsupervised team from Holland.

For the Hearts lads it was a great experience, particularly as they played against a South American team, amongst other foreign opposition. Unfortunately we never won a game but our keeper was awarded a nickname which reflected his running style – Olive Oyle! Poor Micky Watters kicked the ground in the final minute of the last game, sustaining a fracture in his foot, which put a damper on his career at Hearts.

The grim surroundings of the Dinamo Bucharest stadium. Bullet holes are visible around what we were told was a sniper's window in the overlooking building; Brighton and Hove Albion FC are warming up in the foreground.

Meals in the town hall for the 20 teams proved to be a great feat of catering. Certain technical staff had a table on the stage, the Russians among them, and with the open market not fully available to citizens of the USSR, it was sad but interesting to see the sauces, mustards and condiments disappearing into briefcases to begin an unexpected journey beyond the Iron Curtain.

There was something of a carnival atmosphere in the town after Benfica won the final, which led to us getting back to the dormitory/gymnasium a little later than usual. On entering we found a scene of pillage – everyone's gear had been rifled through, including my own. Maxie Christie (son of Terry Christie, then manager of the now defunct Meadowbank Thistle FC) exclaimed: 'They stole ma denim jaiket, ma mother will kill me!'

When the dust had settled we found that Tony's holdall had been taken as a swag bag along with all his smart clothes. Much to his embarrassment, he returned to Scotland carrying what was left in a black rubbish bag. Hearts had been tanned on and off the pitch.

On the coach back to Bruxelles airport, word filtered through to us that the Hearts chairman, Wallace Mercer, had announced he would attempt to merge the two top Edinburgh clubs in order to compete more effectively against Celtic and Rangers. This was a stunning piece of news. For the press it was manna from heaven. During the close season a dog biting a postman would be newsworthy. This was dynamite.

The older heads on the bus realised how our good friends in Leith would react. Many Hearts supporters were not in favour as they, like their Hibs counterparts, enjoyed four derby matches every season. As we all know, it never happened, but the attempt aroused many 'sleeping' Hibees. The ensuing campaign to save the Easter Road club from the merger killed off the notion of Edinburgh becoming a one-club city for another generation. Without becoming embroiled in an argument over the issue, I feel it is the only way to crack the Old Firm hegemony. 'Edinburgh is the Capital but Glasgow has the capital' and neither of the two Edinburgh clubs can compete financially with the Old Firm on their own, although Jim Jefferies in his second stint as Hearts manager in 2011 deserves great credit for hanging onto their coat tails for so long.

The pre-season 90–91 preparations were straight out of the football directors' manual, *How Not to Prepare a Side for the Scottish Premier League*. One mistake was sending the team to an impoverished, post-revolutionary country. About six months before, on Christmas Day 1989, President Ceausescu and his wife had been executed by firing squad. And so when I learned that a visit to Romania for matches on two consecutive days had been arranged as part of our busy training schedule, I wondered if the club knew what it was letting itself in for.

I ran through my physio hamper checklist: adhesive felt; antiseptic cream and liquid; antiseptic wipes; aspirin; bandage scissors; blister patches; chiropody kit; cold spray; cotton wool; deep heat rub; EAB (elastic adhesive bandage); eye bath; fleecy web; fabric elastoplast; ibuprofen tabs; inhaler; Me-Fix; nasal spray; non-adherent dressings; oil (a mix of vegetable oil and methyl salicylate); paracetamol; players' individual orthotics; pliers/leatherman/Swiss army knife; saline pods;

scissors (sharp/blunt); silicone heel pads and toe separators; soap (bars and liquid); talcum powder; Tubigrip (three sizes); Tubifoam (for toes); vaseline; Vic VapoRub.

It took the Gatwick bus 10 minutes to find the Romanian plane which had been chartered to take Hearts and Brighton FC to Bucharest. The shabby appearance of the plane stunned the players, who were used to better things. The feeling that the arrangements were somewhat ad hoc was confirmed when, mid-flight, we were informed that we would be landing in Brussels to pick up RFC Liège. Could we perhaps take our minds off the prolonged flight and console ourselves with the in-flight service? No chance. The sandwiches, like the carpets, were turning up at the corners. I could see that Romania was not going to be a picnic.

Bucharest was dominated by the ugly, monolithic buildings favoured by the ex-dictator. We were installed in a multi-, and I mean *multi*-storey hotel, and swiftly learned that catering was not this establishment's strong point. The only available drinking water – which came in bottles of all colours, shapes and sizes – had a little sediment or pond life mixed in for good measure. We would have done well to take a tip from the cast and crew of *The African Queen* – to avoid amoebic dysentry, Hepburn, Bogart and Huston opted to drink nothing but alcohol while filming on location in the Congo.

In short order, most of the Hearts squad succumbed to appalling diarrhoea. My own remedy was to stop eating in order to give my digestive tract a rest, but footballers have to eat and drink in order to function as performing athletes. The hampers we had brought with us mainly contained dry, high carb fare, such as biscuits and cornflakes, and liquid was required but it seemed that good fresh water was not to be had.

Dinamo Bucharest very hospitably had gifts for us all. I hate to sound ungrateful, but where they managed to acquire such a collection of glassware had us all beat, as the shops were totally bare. It happened that Derek Ferguson, who was making his debut for Hearts after transferring from Rangers for £750,000, was selected as Player of the Competition. He was presented with a particularly hideous blood red vase, at least a metre in height. It was going to be a challenge to get this creation back to Edinburgh, but it arrived in better shape than most of the players.

Two draws against Liège and Brighton can be seen as a triumph considering the alimentary problems which handicapped the Jambos. Somewhere along the way the Liège boys had needled the Hearts. We all felt they had a tip about themselves. At any rate, retribution was delivered at the farewell dinner. The hotel chef, who apparently prided himself on his desserts, must have been appalled to discover that the last thing on the lads' minds was tucking into the sweet course. This sumptuous, creamy flan was served in individual card containers. As soon as the speeches were over, boss Alex MacDonald picked up his helping and, holding it on the palm of his hand, nodded to the team that they should do likewise. On a count of three, they all hurled these missiles at the Belgian team, who reciprocated with a volley in kind. Proceedings descended into the sort of fun and games you'd expect in a Laurel and Hardy movie.

Working in hospitals means I have seen more than my share of ill people but take it from me, at the airport the next day the Hearts squad resembled a crop of zombies. They would not have been out of place in a mortuary.

In addition to the souvenirs presented to us by our hosts, a bundle of Romanian currency – the leu – had been given to every member of the party. Each bundle stood about a foot in height and was supposedly worth a hundred pounds sterling. Scott Crabbe, Robbo's strike partner, being a generous soul, offered his to an elderly couple who were sitting nearby. After looking around for secret policemen, they grabbed the dough and did a bunk.

Back in Edinburgh, we had 48 hours to prepare for a two-match visit to Valencia, which had been organised through the Mittens (father and son). Charlie Mitten was a maverick winger for Manchester United, before and after WWII; later he played in Colombia for Independiente Santa Fe, and came to be known as 'The Bogotá Bandit'. Despite his class on the field – he scored 61 goals for Man United – he never did represent his country.

In Valencia we were put up in a motel on an industrial estate, fine for commercial travellers but hardly suitable for the Hearts. Before the first match a prestigious lunch was laid on by our host. Because the bus to training was delayed, a timely arrival proved impossible. We arrived an hour late. Alex ducked out of the lunch, leaving Wattie B. and me to face a frosty reception from the Valencians. Noticing how discomfited I was, Charlie Mitten tried to assure me that our late arrival would not be taken as a slight but my toes were still curling in my shoes when the paella arrived, understandably not at its best.

The subterranean dressing room at the Estadio Mestalla was like a sauna, even in the evening. I was concerned because I had not fully recovered from the Bucharest trip and felt that I might not be able to fulfil my duties to the team as a result. And of course I knew that many of them would be below par. That night I learned why there was a bat on Valencia's logo – the stadium was infested by them. Despite scoring first through John Colquhoun, we were beaten 3-1.

By the time the second game came round everyone was suffering from the cumulative effects of this and the previous trip. Alex's instructions to the boys were just to keep the ball and stop Levante from scoring. This they duly did, the game ending goalless.

As we were boarding for the flight home the following day, one of the players was whistling merrily as he stowed his hand luggage. A rather snooty lady pronounced in a stage whisper, 'Eh just cenn't stend whistling!' At that, a spontaneous team effort kicked in with the dawn chorus blasting through economy class.

Shortly after our return to Scotland, Alex had a a an 'end of pre-season' staff get-together at the Marine Hotel in North Berwick, which was used regularly as a hide-away prior to big matches. This particular evening had a valedictory feel to it and I wonder now if Alex had got a whiff of what was to come.

With a league defeat against Dunfermline and a League Cup quarter-final defeat against Aberdeen, the season did not start well. However one humorous moment sticks in my mind. After a poor performance against Rangers, the small players' lounge at Tynecastle was full. Enter

Terry Hurlock, a tenacious wing-half who had the same ruthless streak as Souness. 'Not a bad day's work. Lookin' forward to good naht out in GlasGOWE wif a monkey in me back pocket!' he announced. At which one of the many WAGs present piped up, with an accent straight from Govan Cross: 'Whit aboot him then, sez he's goat a donkey in his back poaket.' This was greeted with howls of laughter but did nothing to soften the effects of a sore defeat.

The following Monday I was busy as usual in the physio's room, the place still resembling a clearing station with bodies, kit and all sorts of paraphernalia scattered around, when Alex walked in, right hand outstretched: 'That's me, I've been sacked,' he said, thanked me for my support, then turned and disappeared.

I didn't meet him again until a fateful cup-tie at Broomfield when I found out how fickle and partisan relationships in professional football can be. Joe Jordan was about five months into his stewardship of Hearts when the third round Scottish cup-tie against the Airdrieonians – now managed by Alex – loomed large. It had been decided that it would be down to me, the great multi-tasker, to take the kit over to Broomfield and lay it out while the lads had a meal and a chance to relax pre-match on this biting cold day. Fine, I was always happier being busy than sitting around shooting the breeze.

Broomfield was never one of the most hospitable grounds. The visitors' dressing room was small and there was hardly space for the kit hampers. They were deposited outside the door and Mr Scott, our driver, returned to Bothwell, leaving me with the simple task of finding the groundsman, who would have a key to let me in. You've guessed it, he was out to lunch. I thought that was plausible. The smell of rat was not yet in the air. Some time passed before I saw Alex approaching, accompanied by his long-time scout, coach and analyst, John Binnie. 'Any chance I can get into this dressing room?' I said hopefully, as I was getting a little colder with each passing minute. Somehow I sort of knew what the response would be. 'Naw, the groundsman's goat the key an' he's away fur his denner,' came the reply from Alex, who passed me without breaking stride.

Should auld acquaintance be forgot? Aye, right.

Was it naive of me to expect some sympathetic handling from old workmates? I was no further forward by the time the team arrived – at which point the groundsman materialised to open the door. But the damage to the team's preparations had been accomplished. From the Hearts point of view, to complain would have been a sign of weakness and Joe, as manager, was certainly not a man to kow-tow, nothing was said.

Hearts were never going to get a result that day. Gary Mackay scored first but Airdrie ground out a 2-1 victory, a pattern, strangely enough, which would be played out over the following three seasons, Airdrieonians becoming Hearts' nemesis.

Going back to September 1990, Sandy Clark found himself in charge for a couple of games in the interregnum between MacDonald and Jordan. He and his No. 2, Hearts wing half David McCreery (the former Manchester United, Newcastle United and Northern Ireland internationalist), set about plotting the downfall of Dnipro Dnipropetrovsk when they were drawn against them in the UEFA Cup.

In preparation for the clash in the Ukraine, the Hearts board had pulled off a master stroke by acquiring the high-powered services of Tim Kelly, an experienced hotelier and a troubleshooter for a large hotel group. He was given responsibility for everything that went down our throats. The trip organiser, Ian Dinwiddie, also recruited a Russian-speaking Liverpudlian who proved indispensable. The efforts made by these guys greatly contributed to the success of the trip.

On the flight out, Kelly acted as a one-man cabin crew, dispensing survival packs and other goodies to players and staff. In Dnepr a hotel had been opened specially for our needs. The players are the main concern and keeping them happy can often come down to something as simple as cornflakes or a jar of marmalade. Kelly didn't have to do much wooing to persuade the kitchen staff to make use of the provisions we had brought, because they were all hoping to bag the leftovers.

As a public relations move, Dinwiddie suggested that the non-playing staff each buy 200 Marlboro cigarettes to distribute as mini-bribes to locals who could be helpful. The ploy opened many doors –

and also closed a few when some locals invaded the hotel in an attempt to flog us some moonshine. 'Here's 20 fags – now Foxtrot Oscar!'

Team selection for the match on the 19th saw Alan McLaren the surprise appointment as captain. In response to this encouragement, the brilliant international player in the making put in a show-stopping performance. Gary Mackay was unfit and Neil Berry sustained a thigh injury early in the game but despite these setbacks, Hearts more than held their own in front of a partisan crowd inside the Meteor Stadium and duly opened the scoring.

George Wright was released in a wide right position and carried the ball well into the hosts' half before delivering a cross to the back post. Wayne Foster played a cushioned header back across the goal where it was met with a diving header from the small, rotund torpedo, John Robertson. Nothing got past young McLaren at centre half, on the ground or in the air, and he proved to be an inspirational figure for his team-mates. Although Dnipro eventually equalised with a curler into Henry Smith's left-hand postage stamp just when it looked as though the big man was going to defy them, it had been a great team effort.

Content in the knowledge we would be emerging from the Ukraine with a healthy result and an excellent chance to progress in the return leg in Edinburgh, we made our way to the team bus. The atmosphere was as you'd expect – well pleased. However I noticed that a hostile crowd was gathering outside and I asked George Wright, who was sitting next to me, to pull down the louvre blinds. No sooner had he done so than the window exploded and a brick hurtled through, narrowly missed George's head. The driver put his foot to the floor and we were soon out of danger but it certainly left the senses scrambled. Maybe we shouldn't have been too surprised. Matches behind the Iron Curtain always presented challenges, both on and off the field.

CHAPTER 6

Falling Short

WHEN JOE JORDAN was in his prime playing years I was working in Kowloon and pretty well starved of top-level football. My rations consisted of Middlesbrough at the Hong Kong National Stadium, where I saw a young Graeme Souness stamp his authority on the Red China players, and Bobby Charlton bringing a select side over to play some exhibition matches.

When I first met Joe in September 1990, I had expected a war horse. What I saw was a thoroughbred, lean and narrow with little upper body enhancement – what he had was all hereditary. At physiotherapy training school, we had been taught to expect speed and range of movement to triumph over strength and bulk. Ali v Liston (Ali beat Liston to win the World Heavyweight Boxing Championship and then defended the title against the same opponent) exemplifies the notion. Added to the speed, Joe had aggression aplenty, which he showed when he played in the occasional reserve match while he was Hearts manager. Marvin Wilson, an apprentice wing half, was to catch an earful when he failed to make a particular run: 'Maaarvin, you're a lazy little baastard!' echoed round the empty terraces. In a testimonial match for Gary Mackay against Everton, Joe scored with a diving header, proving that, at 40 years of age, the desire was still there.

Some weeks prior to this change of management, Hearts had travelled to Aberdeen to play in a League Cup tie, and some of the players had indulged in the hospitality offered by the home team after the match. Maybe it was comfort eating, as Hearts had been soundly beaten. Scott Crabbe, a fine 'home grown' striker, wasn't even on the bench for the match; doubly 'down in the dumps', he may have consumed twice as many of the infected sandwiches as anyone else. The next day a few of the squad were unwell but Scott was extremely sick. Salmonella was diagnosed and his weight plummeted.

An illness like this is unusual in young footballers. When the acute phase had passed and Scott was getting back some of his normal *joie de vivre*, I decided to introduce a little light training. To get away from prying eyes we went up to Comiston Park, where we walked a little, jogged a little and, in between, shot the breeze. At about 10pm that night I took a phone call from a distressed Crabbo. 'Al, ah'm in agony, ah cannae stan' on ma feet!' Oh boy, just a slight thrill of panic traversed my lower bowel. When we managed to stretcher him into the club for examination, we concluded that the illness had starved the muscles of so much nutrition, they could not support the joints. The arches of the feet had collapsed, causing intense pain – there are 33 joints in each foot, every one requiring support – and for once the over-used phrase 'I'm in agony' was an apt description of what was being experienced. With some electrical stimulation, localised exercises and advice from a dietician, Scott began the second stage of his recovery. Hearts, meantime, were deprived of the services of a valuable striker.

Having a manager who had played in Italy added spice to the next round of the UEFA Cup, which paired Hearts with Bologna – not the most glamorous team, but Italian nevertheless. The first leg was at home and the Italians arrived in some style. No club blazers and flannels for them – camel hair matching jackets, no less, with each garment costing more than I earned in a week! Perhaps the dingy surroundings of Tynecastle upset their Latin sensibilities. Hearts looked good for a 3-0 victory, although an away goal for the out-of-sorts visitors took the shine off the result.

For the away leg Hearts stayed in the Hotel Molino Rosso which had been specially built for Italia '90. It is my recollection that one of the Arab nations had paid for its construction and it was the first time I had seen energy-saving lights controlled by photo-electric cells. Crabbo was included in the party as he had resumed training and was back to his chirpy self, on one occasion before a meal shouting, 'Gaffer, whut diz *al dente* mean?'

The Stadio Renata Dall'Ara, where Mussolini had once orated to vast crowds, was approached via a tunnel which seemed endless, as we had to carry a huge kit hamper along it. I blamed Sandy Clark, now relegated to first team and youth team coach, for buying this sarcophagus, but in fairness, we didn't expect to be so far from the stadium. The match itself was a let-down for everyone, with the away goal proving critical. The Italians ran out 4-3 aggregate winners.

It wasn't a total disaster though, as Gary Mackay managed to buy a rather fine coat.

In a new manager's first season miracles rarely happen and this was the case with Joe Jordan. The club was stable but Europe was off the radar and a serious injury to defensive midfielder Neil Berry cast a cloud over Tynecastle. A friendly against Arbroath was arranged for Gayfield in February to allow some match practice after a rocky spell in cup and league. Knee injuries often at first appear innocuous and they can happen in a fraction of a second. In Neil's case the effects were career threatening. Cruciate ligament damage was now recognised early and the danger of attempting rehabilitation on unstable knees was a thing of the past. Early in my NHS career patients would be referred to the physiotherapy department for 'provocative exercises' in order to confirm that a cartilage was damaged. The accompanying prescription card from the consultant frequently had 'IDK' written on it to indicate 'Internal Derangement of Knee' (more cynical types in my business would interpret this as 'I Don't Know'). Yes, things have got better.

Neil had been through the orthopaedic wringer many times. An ankle injury had seen him hospitalised at the Princess Margaret Rose Hospital, where, following the surgery, a junior registrar had advised him to find another career. That night I paid Neil a visit and found him visibly upset, believing his career to be over. Reassurance was the order of the day and I encouraged him to wait and speak to the consultant before accepting this opinion. 'That was the organ grinder's monkey who spoke to you, wait until you see the organ grinder!' I told him.

Footballers' joints often have an unnatural appearance, showing wear and tear more typical of older joints. Younger muscles absorb much of the load and only as the player approaches middle age do the crows come home to roost, 'the crows' being painful osteoarthritis, a condition characterised by the erosion of the joint surfaces. Much of physiotherapy is supportive during long-term rehabilitation. Encouragement, guidance, patience and in some cases authority are laid on the line. In Neil I had a model patient: after being shown the routine with an explanation of the whys and the wherefores, he demonstrated great motivation over the next nine months. On regaining full fitness he had a long slog in the reserves. His attitude was never in doubt but in spite of receiving glowing reports from Sandy Clark, the manager left him out of his first team plans.

After successfully splitting the Old Firm in season 91–92, Hearts qualified for Europe – a great achievement to crown Joe and Frank's first full year in charge. In a different era, that second position in the SPL would have put the Jambos in the Champions League, which has always been a cut above the UEFA tournament.

Hearts having been drawn away in the first leg against Slavia, the Tynecastle faithful would have to make a fairly short trip to Prague. (I was to discover in later years that one of my uncles was buried in the Prague Military Cemetery after having been taken prisoner during the fall of Crete; with the war almost won, he was killed in an Allied bombing raid.) The hotel we stayed in was one used by the politburo and communist trade unionists. Overlooking the city, it was, in its Eastern Bloc way, quite a comfortable billet. There were no hints of conspiracies at training, just the usual gesticulations that our period of practice time had elapsed.

The match was one of Graeme Hogg's best for the club. Not having either 'Big Boy' McLaren or Craig Levein for support stirred him into reprising his former role as a centre back at Manchester United. He had an ex-Aberdeen player alongside, Dutchman Peter Van de Ven, a player who, I felt, never really took to life at Tynecastle. I got the impression of someone who just did enough and little more. Perhaps he had retirement or a return to the Low Countries on his mind. Like most quality European players he looked after himself and kept clear of injuries. Incidentally, it was his persistence that prodded the board into buying an ice machine (one did exist but it served the sponsors' lounge and provided me with ice during the week). At any rate, along with the inspired goalkeeping of Henry Smith, Hogg and Van de Ven kept the score to one goal against.

The return leg was a torrid affair under Tynecastle's notoriously poor floodlights. Despite the visitors having a man sent off, the tie was finely balanced until Glynn Snodin, a shrewd, left-sided full back, scored with a magnificent free kick which put the tie to bed. Hearts moving on to the next round, having won 4-3.

Standard Liège had been Hearts' first opponents in Europe in 1958, the occasion being the European Cup. Thirty-five years later both teams were to meet again in the next round of the UEFA competition, with the Maroons hoping to avenge Liège's earlier 6-3 aggregate reverse (against a Hearts side which had scored an astonishing 132 goals, with only 29 against, in season 57–58). Liège, an affluent if not prepossessing university town on the River Meuse, is sometimes called 'the capital city of gun-makers'. (Its tradition in gunsmithing is something I first learned of when visiting the site of the Battle of Chickamauga in Tennessee, where I came across one of the city's products – a cannon.)

The first leg was a stuffy affair at Tynecastle, Hearts unluckily losing 1-0. In the return Hearts had a lot of the game but, as so often happens when on top, if you don't score the other lot will. A goal from the Belgians saw them progress 2-0 on aggregate. Jimmy Murray, a fine free-scoring inside forward who had played in the previous ties of 58, witnessed Liège winning again, although by a lesser margin. (A little bit of Hearts history here: Jimmy was the first ever Scotsman to score a goal in the World Cup, in Sweden in 1958. I met him on several occasions during my time at Hearts as we had a mutual friend in Jimmy McGregor, a physiotherapist who worked at Goodison Park and Old Trafford. When I was a student, Jimmy Mac was working with Bruce Hay, the No. 1 physio at Clyde FC, and after Murray joined them I was often regaled with tales of his time at Shawfield.)

While Joe Jordan was in charge I got to know his assistant, Frank Connor, quite well. This was a guy who had had his fair share of ups and downs during his career in football. He had been a goalkeeper in his playing days and while his height nowadays would have limited his prospects, in the post-war era being below average height was not necessarily a handicap – Jocky Robertson of Third Lanark and Roy Henderson of Queen of the South come to mind.

After training, Frank would spend considerable time showering and fine tuning his appearance. Then he would step down into the physio's room, which was adjacent to the referees' room and also doubled as a refuge for the management. (It had the best shower in the place at that time, unlike the 'shower' who used it on match days.)

There would follow an extended monologue on one man's experience of the game. Frank had worked with Jock Stein and Jock Wallace and at times it was difficult to tell which 'Big Jock' he was on about. On one occasion he was particularly scathing about John Millar's choice of skin cream, Oil of Ulay being his chosen product. Yes, footballers do have a feminine side! So we all had a right good laugh when it was noticed that there was a family size tub of Nivea in Frank's toilet bag, enough for a hundred babies' bottoms. The contents of Frank's training kit pockets, which he often failed to empty, would go through the washing machine, rosary beads and crucifixes being no exception – I remarked one day that he should have been called Francis the Baptist!

Frank's contribution was enormous. Because of him, in training, the Jambos began to look like a professional outfit. Instead of it being a free-for-all, each player had initialled gear, the colours alternating: blue one day, red the next. Frank's appetite for the game was enormous but unfortunately he was on the wrong side of 50 to help his manager with the physical side of training. This meant that the boss could not distance himself from the squad and being hands-on can mean that a view of the broader spectrum is lost.

Frank's contacts within the game allowed Hearts to arrange two pre-season camps at Dingwall, enjoying Ross County's hospitality, but the contrast between Joe and Frank's training methods could not have been greater – hardly surprising. The influence on Joe of Leeds United, Manchester United and AC Milan had to surface. Injuries in training under his regimen were rare. I suspect that had Frank been given free rein, the incidence would have been greater. Stein and Wallace had been shaped by the methods of the post-war years and the military hangover prevailed well into the 1990s. This approach certainly got players fit but there were casualties along the way. Sports Science was still seen as an oxymoron. At a lecture given by Jerry Gilmore, an eminent surgeon who specialised in repairing the 'sportsman's hernia', I learned that the work he received from Arsenal FC dried up after Arsène Wenger took over. A different approach had led to a huge reduction in the incidence of hernia – certainly good for Arsenal's players but not so beneficial for Mr Gilmore's bank balance. Gilmore introduced a little levity to the proceedings, showing a slide of a rhinoceros and asking what this beast had in common with a Harley Street surgeon. Answer: they are thick-skinned, horny and charge a lot!

Injuries did occur though. Ian Ferguson, a centre forward signed on Frank's recommendation from Raith Rovers, was a striker who ran onto the ball, thriving on passes along the 'gulley' (the channel on either side of the centre forward position), as David McCreery, ex Manchester and Newcastle United, called it. Ian didn't like, or wasn't adept, at receiving the ball with his back to the opposition's goal. Joe and Frank hammered the ball at him after training and he was expected to control it when it arrived, hold it up and lay it off. This wasn't in Ian's locker and consequently he picked up an inner thigh strain from the constant lifting and rotating of his thigh and leg, which did nothing for the lad's confidence. Perhaps looking at the good things in his game would have been more appropriate. He clearly had a striker's reflexes, as shown by a magnificent half-volley against Celtic. During a lull in training the following week he was asked to reproduce this wonderful strike. After numerous failed attempts, we decided just to enjoy the moment on video.

One wet Saturday at Tynecastle there must have been a frustrating period in the game as the manager was becoming more and more agitated. The pitch at Tynie during the early '90s was surrounded by triangular advertising hoardings held in place by sandbags. Not very sophisticated but they brought in much-needed revenue. Giving vent to this frustration, Joe swung his tried and tested left foot at the hoarding in front of him, knocking it several feet forward. The match ended satisfactorily. The following week, while I was absorbed in my work with injured players, the manager appeared, something of a rarity unless he suspected someone was malingering.

'I've done something to my foot. I don't know what it is. Can you have a look at it?'

Well, I knew what was wrong. I asked him if he remembered blootering the advertising board. 'That can't have caused this,' he responded.

Very rarely do professionals 'toe-poke' the ball – it is either 'the laces' or the inside or the outside of the boot – but in this case the manager had a severe contusion of both joints in his big toe. His involvement in the game had presumably overcome any immediate discomfort.

In the '93 Scottish Cup semi-final against Rangers at Parkhead, luck was to play a telling part in the result. With Derek Ferguson dominating the midfield for Hearts, the Jambos took the lead through Allan Preston getting his head on the end of a John Robertson cross. The Jam Tarts looked comfortable defending this advantage when a wayward shot at the Hearts goal was deflected wide by a Rangers player's backside. The referee made a poor decision by awarding a corner to the Teddies instead of a goal kick to the Jambos. From this corner Dave McPherson, the former Hearts centre back, equalised after 'a stramash in the goal mouth'. This lucky break led to another. John Brown, the Rangers midfielder, sclaffed a clearance with his shin which Ally McCoist controlled adroitly, ran on and despatched the ball past goalkeeper Nicky Walker. Hearts tried hard to get back into the game but the deck was stacked against them in another losing semi.

Joe and Frank were sacked but to their credit they had built on Alex and Sandy's legacy by establishing a youth policy, and bringing parts of the stadium used by the players into the modern era.

CHAPTER 7

Madrid and Belgrade

FROM SPLITTING THE Old Firm in the previous season, the slump to mid-table mediocrity in season 92–93 was hard to bear for the fans. Still, there was no threat of relegation, which had continued to haunt me as failure to remain in the top flight would mean cut-backs, with physiotherapists high on the list of non-priorities.

Hearts had qualified for Europe thanks to a fifth-place finish and the unexpected cash was welcome. Crowds had been dwindling and it occurred to me that perhaps a more adventurous approach was needed to give the edge to matches at Tynecastle.

The luck of the draw still existed, which meant that this secondary competition could match the minnows against the mighty. It's highly unlikely that Inter Milan or Bayern Munich will ever play Hearts again in a meaningful competition but the supporters must have been reasonably pleased when a home tie against Atlético Madrid was announced. The city of Madrid showed some interest – probably the novelty for them was being paired with another capital, albeit of a small nation. The Spanish TV companies came to town and took over the ground and while there were cables everywhere, the revenue from advertising alone must have pleased the board and helped make up for any associated inconvenience.

The afternoon before the match the señors arrived to lay out kit and generally prepare, but it soon became apparent that paranoia ruled in their camp. I was pestered to supply keys for the dressing room. They insisted, despite my assurances that they didn't need to lock it, and were given the ubiquitous No. 125 key which opened just about everything except the door leading into the tunnel. What was all the fuss about? After they left I went for a nosey. I could turn the key in the lock but couldn't open the door – our visitors had barricaded the doorway, floor to ceiling, with kit hampers and surplus baggage. They were a strange lot.

The match at Tynecastle was a shade disappointing. Losing a late goal meant that a result in Madrid with Sandy Clark's makeshift team, which had old and new players trying to gel, was odds against. The Spaniards would be happy with a 2-1 away loss. In Madrid we were again put up in one of the finest central hotels. Accommodation was never skimped on when venturing abroad competitively (as opposed to pre-season). The only downside was that the Blues Brothers – McNeil and Logan – tanned my mini-bar (alcohol was removed from the players' rooms as a matter of course).

No trip to Madrid would be complete without a visit to Real's ground. I particularly remember the Estadio Santiago Bernabéu trophy room, where even the smallest exhibit was carefully catalogued; it was twice the size of the Brown gymnasium at Tynecastle. But I was never happy about players hanging around, putting weight through their legs when they could be resting. In Jordan's time, when the team were in the south of France preparing for a cup-tie, we were visiting Monaco's stadium when I mentioned that players should really get back to the hotel as they were training twice a day. Wallace Mercer took the point and immediately pulled the plug on the visit.

As we were touring Real's stadium, Kevin Thomas was seen peering around and then scrutinising his tickets for the evening's match. 'I wonder where my parents will be sitting?' quoth he. Sandy enlightened him: 'If they're sitting here they're no' gonnae see much of the gemme!' An Edinburgh lad, Kevin was a gifted, natural striker who had been nurtured by Sandy. During his time at Hearts he made us all laugh either by actions or words. Another occasion which springs to mind was when he made an entrance into a west end restaurant in the capital, looked around imperiously, spotted Dave McPherson at one of the tables and called over to the big man: 'David, we must do lunch!' He had a habit of opening a conversation with 'Whabooeh' (What aboot...eh...) This was seized upon by Craig Levein and John Robertson who changed his name from Kevin the Legend to Waabooeh.

If a player had a meeting with a consultant I always tried to accompany him. This could speed up the process of rehabilitation in that I didn't have to wait for a written report. Kevin had an appointment with an eminent consultant orthopaedic surgeon one day. We entered the examination room and the consultant invited him to lie on the couch and remove his trousers. This he did. We were then confronted with the meat and two veg, completely commando, bollock naked from the waist down – for an ankle examination!

There was a moat around the pitch at the Vicente Calderón Stadium – this I discovered when retrieving balls from behind the goals at the training session the night before the match with Atlético. Another thing which caught my eye was the state of the seating, with many of the slabs of concrete loose and broken. At a Scottish ground it was unlikely the police would allow a game to go ahead until the terraces were safe. 'Below decks' things were different. The dressing room was spacious, well ventilated and had several WCs. There was a clinic and a mini operating theatre with an X-ray suite adjacent. Hearts would avail themselves of these facilities after the match.

As I followed the team out of the tunnel I noticed a groundsman sitting on a wee stool, all agog, rubbing his hands together in anticipation. Small memories, why do they stick in one's mind? Is it just our humanity that makes commonplace actions memorable?

Eventually we got a 3-0 'seeing-to' from Los Colchoneros. I was on the pitch after Henry Smith had accidentally punched Craig on the side of the face. It was a classic scenario for a broken cheek bone but Craig was having none of it and completed the match, as did Scott Leitch, our left-sided wing half, despite taking a nasty kick on the crown of his head in the second half, which drew blood. A lad who is kind to dumb animals and old ladies, on the pitch Dr Jekyll becomes Mr Hyde and he was enraged by what had happened. Injuries involving blood had not assumed the present-day pernicketiness of approach and as I tended to him – which was difficult, as he was looking around for the opponent who had inflicted this wound on him – an Atlético player took the water bottle out of my bag. Scott was grabbing at the bottle and attempting to put a wrist lock on the player. The Spaniard took a drink, dropped it and departed with the phrase: 'Bastardo Escoces'. I had to laugh. So much for the community of European nations.

As we licked our wounds afterwards I took some consolation in the fact that the casualties had been taken care of on-site, in sterile surroundings.

Two players come to mind whenever I think of the next competitive foray in Europe: John Colquhoun and Gilles Rousset. Both had played in the Scottish Cup Final a few months earlier, in May 1996, when John had scored a very smart goal to take a little of the shine from Rangers' lollipop. The situation was different for the tall Frenchman, however, as he'd had all summer to sit and stew over Rangers' second goal. For a man so professional and proud, a ball going through his legs and into the net rendered him inconsolable. I can still see him in the Hampden

A long stretch for Gilles Rousset.

dressing room, head in hands, tears running down his cheeks. The runner-up medal was stotted off the wall and I don't know if it was ever retrieved. Two goals down at half time gave Rangers a massive advantage inasmuch as they could sit back and 'pick off' Hearts as the Jambos pressed forward. A 5-1 loss in a cup final was hard to bear.

With Hearts having made the Ibrox outfit work for their league title – dropping six points against the Jambos had made the run-in less than comfortable – putting Hearts to the sword must have given Walter Smith a degree of satisfaction. The greatest sadness on the day was the loss of Gary Locke with a serious knee injury. This would have been the lad's finest hour and to be removed from the field on a stretcher ten minutes into the match was tragic both for Gary and his family.

I had mixed feelings about the venue for Hearts in the first round of the Cup-Winners' Cup. We were matched against Red Star Belgrade. A trip to the Balkans in their present state of flux would have definite edge. Founded just after WWII, Red Star Belgrade was a famous club with many domestic trophies. They had won the European Cup in the early '90s and were clearly one of Europe's finest sides. At Edinburgh Airport I looked at the squad gathered in the departure lounge – Robertson, McPherson, Fulton, Lawrence, Mackay, Naysmith, Rousset, Frail, Goss, Weir, Colquhoun, Hogarth, Cameron, McKenzie, Locke, Ritchie, McManus, Bruno and Thomas – and I thought that this was as good a squad as Hearts had ever taken to a European competition.

Hearts had managed to secure one of Belgrade's finest hotels. We wanted for nothing. Red Star's Crvena Zvezda stadium was massive – but for a small, covered area it would have been a true amphitheatre.

On the night before the game, after training, the management team was visited by a famous former player who had made a name for himself in Scotland. It was Ivan Golac who, as manager, had led Dundee United to victory against Rangers in the Scottish Cup Final. He had played for Red Star's rivals, Partizan, and spent several years with Southampton, where he became a big favourite with the Dell faithful. That affection was mutual. Golac spoke of his happy times there on many occasions. He was no longer involved in management and was now running a chocolate factory; maybe he needed a little sweetness in his life after leaving Gotham City (a name given to the city of Dundee by non-residents). I wasn't privy to the information on Red Star he gave JJ and BB (Jefferies and Brown) but it was sure to have been valuable, coming from a man of such calibre.

With a defence marshalled by experienced cookies like Bruno and McPherson, chances were going to be few for Red Star. In goal, Hearts had a man on a mission in Rousset. After the howler three months earlier, Gilles would be on his mettle. His pride and self-respect were damaged but here was a chance to erase this bitter memory. John Colquhoun had been given a guerrilla role playing up front on his own and his pace was likely to be a concern for the opposing defence.

All went according to plan. Gilles was fantastic, the defence was sound and JC ran himself to a standstill chasing across Red Star's back line. Naturally we were all pleased with the 0-0 result but on happy occasions there is usually something to spoil the party. It came, sure enough, with a blockage and an overflow of the plumbing system in the shower area.

The WC was a hole in the floor with two foot imprints to accommodate the squatter's feet, not an unusual system in southern Europe or in the Far East. This one went seriously wrong. We were ankle deep in kak. Everyone just wanted to get out of this sewer as quickly as possible but here was Pasquale Bruno standing in front of the only mirror, quite unperturbed by the faecal environment, applying his eye make-up. The moment was typically Bruno-esque.

CHAPTER 8
Hydrotherapy

WHEN THE CLUB'S hot seat was entrusted to Sandy Clark after Jordan's sacking in 1993, there is no doubt that he succeeded in his main task of keeping Hearts in the Premier League, thereby enhancing its attractions as a commercial proposition, and at the end of season the team were rewarded with a trip to Canada. Meanwhile Wallace Mercer sold the club to businessman Chris Robinson and solicitor Leslie Deans. On their return to Scotland, Sandy and Hugh McCann were shown the door and, despite having guided the club from the dark days of the '80s to a revival in the '90s, vice chairman Pilmar Smith soon followed. Retaining him in a non-executive role would have been a smart move but the view might have been that someone so close to the previous owner had to go. Similarly, I think that Sandy was perceived as being too close to the previous board. The club secretary Les Porteous was retained as he had all the 'inside track' which the incoming executives had to 'download'. These three guys had kept Hearts afloat, preventing the team sliding into a pantomime outfit, part-time and a fixture in the lower divisions. Like Moses, Wallace was never to see the 'Promised Land' where Hearts would land a major trophy – how he would have loved to have been on that bus down The Mound after the Cup success.

For me, this was something of an unsettling period. By joining Hearts on a full-time basis I had burned my bridges with the NHS and I feared what the next knock on the door would bring. You can imagine my relief, therefore, when Chris Robinson came through to the treatment area to inform me that I would not be following the management out of the door with a UB40 in my hand.

Prior to this sea-change the club had made steps into the modern era with some basic improvements to the players' side of the grandstand. The manager's office was moved from being stuck between the physio's room and the gents' public lavatory to a more appropriate site adjacent to the secretary's office. This was good news as it meant more space for rehab. James Clydesdale, a director of the club and a master builder, was behind these alterations. He was approachable and always open to suggestions, even from a layman like me.

The old bath, which was like a small swimming pool, gave way to a bank of impact showers which offered a more economical and hygienic method of keeping players clean and healthy. There had been a sauna, once considered beneficial for easing tired and painful bodies after training and matches but which actually led to further dehydration – the complete opposite of what a recovering athlete required. Only now was it becoming recognised how crucial rehydration was in accelerating the recovery process after exercise and in athletic conditioning generally. Before one pre-season training session, I was filling a keg with a solution of one of the 'athletic drinks' of the day so that the players could maintain their hydration levels when a coach, who I will not name and shame, told me to leave it at the club as he didn't believe in 'that kind of shite'. It wasn't the only time that enlightenment coming from a mere physiotherapist was laughed off the park.

Rehabilitation in football was no longer couch-bound: it embraced the injured as total beings. At clinics in my early career every cubicle had an infra-red lamp. Use of this type of heat often made up 30 to 40 per cent of the treatment session, very comforting for the patient but not cost-effective and of dubious therapeutic value. At a professional football club the recovery process was strengthened by ensuring that the uninjured parts were kept in top condition. The guys who had long-term injuries were subjected to a six-day week, with Sundays usually reserved for Saturday's casualties. It is now quite rare for any player under 30 to quit the game through injury, thanks mainly to the advance of diagnostic expertise, surgical technique and rehabilitation skills.

The manager appointed by the new board was Tommy McLean, soon to be assisted by Eamonn Bannon and Tom Forsyth as first team coach. The popular Walter Kidd became youth coach. Finding a training area was high on Tommy's to-do list. Joe and Frank had used George Watson's playing fields for a spell, an arrangement which lasted until the pupils' parents realised that what they expected their children to have exclusive use of, was being *desecrated* by footballers!

In search of an alternative, Tommy and I drove all over Edinburgh but we drew a blank. (Only since 2004 have Hearts had a dedicated training area, at Heriot-Watt University.) A facility often used by the apprentice professionals was the indoor football pitch at the Scottish and Newcastle Brewery in Fountainbridge, Sean Connery's early stamping ground. In days gone by, the track around Tynecastle had been used but it was pretty hopeless because it was either very hard or very soft – it froze in winter, was dry in summer, and when it rained it turned into red porridge. Training areas were gathered ad hoc. For early conditioning work I had shown Joe Jordan the bridle path surrounding the Braids golf course. He approved and the team used it for pre-season cross-countries. At Gullane we did hill work on 'Murder Hill', a facility popularised among several football teams by the innovative Jock Wallace (the story goes that, while he was manager at Rangers, one player, on first being subjected to his hard training, did half a lap and disappeared down an exit, never to be seen again). The various areas of Roseburn Park close to Tynecastle, if carefully rotated, were capable of being used year-round for ball work. I found it convenient for injured players returning to running functions but it was a public park, with all the drawbacks that involved.

For the physio room I managed to secure a piece of rehab equipment which the players and I would find indispensable over the next ten years. It was made in the USA – I doubt if a poorly manufactured physiotherapy item has ever left that country. It was a horizontal leg press which could be used to exercise the three major joints in the lower limb: hip, knee and ankle. This apparatus was expensive but when compared to a wage bill it was merely a 'non-recurring expense'. All players benefited and Kevin Thomas, Stephen Frail, Gary Locke, Neil MacFarlane and Róbert Tomaschek in particular owed a large part of their recovery to the work they did on this equipment.

The club was looking up without losing its family atmosphere. Tom Forsyth, the manager's buddy, would regularly bring in potatoes, carrots and cauliflower for me from his gardens in the Clyde Valley, gifts I gratefully accepted as my kids were now teenagers with insatiable appetites.

Water has always been a useful medium in which to exercise. Even race-horse trainers have discovered the benefits of having pools in which to rehabilitate thoroughbreds. So-called 'quack' practitioners had often used immersion as part of their regimen, not that I want to go into their use of water in other areas of the body – I will leave that to the reader's imagination.

Fortunately for the Hearts, Edinburgh has several good public swimming pools. The Scottish attitude to celebrities often prevailed. On our arrival at these amenities, I steeled myself for the inevitable 'ah kent his faither' greeting. Taking recognisable players into the public domain and swimming with the great about-to-be-washed had its moments: 'Jambos in the watter, that's a first, soap dodgin' bastards!' and other such comments flowed freely. Nevertheless the plusses outweighed the minuses. Players who had not reached the dynamic stage of rehabilitation – running, twisting, jumping, falling down, getting up, etc – all appreciated a break from long sessions in the gym, although that is not to say that hydrotherapy is a dawdle.

Buoyancy aids had improved a lot since the days of water-wings. The latest could be worn like a jacket, leaving the arms and legs free of impediment, allowing the body to aqua-jog or sprint in a fashion close to the real thing without putting the body weight through the lower limb joints, which were supported and resisted by the water. However, as in all walks of life, there are the 'Hielan dancers' (chancers). For them, during cardio-vascular work, the floats were removed. In order to stay afloat in the deep end they had to jog (no swimming strokes allowed) at three times the normal speed.

There was pressure on me to ensure that these excursions were not seen as an undeserved break – there had been no jollies under Jordan and there were none now. Behaviour, whether good or bad, is never guaranteed at a football club. As you can imagine, there was always an edge to these visits. Decency was of paramount concern. Long shorts and under-briefs or 'centres' were compulsory. Like any ringmaster I was stripped and ready for any lifesaving emergencies, withstanding jibes like 'Steve Ribs' or 'Hercules Unchained' – 'Ah've seen mair meat on a butcher's apron' and 'Is yer missus feeding the ludger?' Ah, the slings and arrows...

Usually there were no children around, though the same couldn't be said for members of the opposite sex, who were plentiful in all shapes and sizes. George Wright and Graeme Hogg were handfuls – George was the man about town, Hoggie was there to enjoy the view. Ogling, smirks and sniggers were kept to a reasonable level in spite of the odd sighting of 'spider's legs' emerging from cozzie elastic.

One incident which springs to mind involved a male swimmer – not the bonniest – who did regular lengths of the pool. George had noticed his eccentric swimming style and how he breathed. Swimming behind this poor lad, George aped all his actions. The other swimmers were in stitches while the target remained oblivious to what was going on.

During one aqua-jog interval session at the Sighthill Diving Pool (a great facility, so deep that there was no chance of the players getting their feet on the bottom), Hoggie was so uncommitted – he was swimming more than jogging – that I had to take him out of the hydrotherapy detail. Amphibian he wasn't and he made no significant effort to make the metamorphosis. Hoggie had come to Hearts from the top of the tree, Manchester United, which had its own private training facilities at The Cliff – to a team which expected him to train in public parks and swimming pools. His perception of any injury seemed to be that he would recover spontaneously, without the use of what he probably saw as primitive physiotherapy services. At Hearts, in the absence of a variety of rehab kit, I placed the emphasis on encouragement and commitment from the players. Their attitude was an essential ingredient to a successful return to fitness.

I have seen pretty horrendous spinal injuries resulting from over-exuberance or misjudgment of the depth of a pool. All of the cases I had involvement with were guys who had just arrived on holiday or servicemen on shore leave who had taken on some local refreshment. Most had dived into the shallow end, the hands and arms meeting with the bottom unexpectedly, before the upper limbs could react, the head following and being forcibly extended on the neck. The spinal cord could be permanently damaged as a result.

This scenario was almost reproduced on one occasion with a Hearts rehab party. For various reasons we ended up going to the Infirmary Street pool instead of Warrender Baths. The players retired to the booths to change and then went for a shower. Barry Keegan happened to be quicker than the rest of us. The set-up at Warrender, with the showers next to the deep end, was reversed at Infirmary Street. Before I could warn him, he had performed a forward roll into three feet of water. If he had made an orthodox dive, he might be a tetraplegic today. Fortunately a scraped nose was all he suffered.

CHAPTER 9

Speed Ball

THE FAMOUS SCOTTISH professional sprinter George McNeil was responsible for the introduction of the speed ball to Hearts' training programme. It was implemented due to the wisdom of the vice chairman Pilmar Smith who had seen its positive effects on professional runners. Along with the speed ball came an efficient, economic conditioning routine – all it required was a chin bar and a set of truncated parallel bars, and these were fitted into the old Brown gymnasium at little expense. Until this innovation the gym had been used almost exclusively for 'head tennis', something that MacDonald was particularly keen on – he took on all comers and thrashed them. This game was a rite of passage for youngsters at the club; the penance exacted by Alex was a pound note signed by the defeated player – he had about 50 of these framed and hung on his office wall.

The gym had been constructed under the grandstand to celebrate King George V's 25th year on the throne. Like many other mementoes, the plaque recording this event has disappeared. (One 'near thing' was the pink and yellow Scotland jersey of one of Scotland's and Hearts' greatest players, Bobby Walker, which was rescued from a bundle of rubbish destined for the tip. If my memory serves me correctly, this jersey – in Lord Roseberry's racing colours, which the Scottish National Football team wore instead of the traditional blue – was worn against England in 1910.)

The exercises we adopted to go along with the speed ball were a variation on a programme developed by Stuart Togher, who had coached several high-profile athletes with a dynamic circuit of burpees, press-ups, 'chins', dips and trunk curls.

All the Hearts players got stuck into this new training approach and, while some did not care for all of the callisthenics, everyone took to the speed ball. In a short space of time youngsters and senior players alike could hit the ball at least 300 times per minute. Hand and eye co-ordination was improved but more importantly the muscles of the neck, upper spine, shoulders and arms were strengthened without the players being aware of what was happening.

When the first team squad were in the gym with half a dozen speed balls in action simultaneously, the noise was deafening. The rhythmic drum-beat that pulsated out onto McLeod Street at first puzzled the locals as there had never been a sound like it before at Tynecastle. Stalwarts like Roddy McDonald, Walter Kidd, Gary Mackay and Neil Berry became speed ball junkies.

During the reign of the 'twa Tams' (McLean and Forsyth) some results were unexpewcted and it could be argued that points gained from the Old Firm that season kept the Jambos in the top flight. The last home match against Celtic took place in late February 1995, when the old School End terracing had been demolished to make way for an all-seated away end. Encounters with Celtic were usually highly entertaining affairs and in my experience forecasting the result was always a gamble. Narrow wins for the home side were more than balanced by runaway victories for the Hoops. This one was going 'against the head' – it looked like being a narrow victory for the away side. A green mesh screen had been erected behind the School End goals and as the game slipped away from the Hearts we could see the faithful trudging slowly out of the ground. For some odd reason this sad trek behind the screens reminded me of scenes I had read about in Solzhenitsyn's *The Gulag Archipelago*.

With minutes to spare Hearts were pressing the opposition's goal, although Celtic were defending a 1-0 lead with some comfort. The ball was cleared to the edge of the penalty box in the direction of Willie Jamieson – a difficult, spinning ball which had the home bench screaming at Willie, 'Take a touch!' Conversely, a shout from the away bench, directed with some derision at the Jambos' management (both ex 'Teddy Bears'), was delivered: 'Hit it, Willie!' Well, Willie chose the

Colin Cameron atop an ecstatic John Robertson after Hearts won the Scottish Cup in 1998.
© Eric McCowat Sports Photo Archive.

Gary Locke bear-hugged by Stevie Fulton who captained the team that brought the Scottish Cup to Tynecastle. © Eric McCowat Sports Photo Archive.

The scene at the Cenotaph, Haymarket, on 'Sair Heid Sunday' following the Scottish Cup win.

Mark De Vries in action v Sunderland FC, 2003. © Eric McCowat Sports Photo Archive.

Steven Pressley after winning against Basel FC, 2004. © Eric McCowat Sports Photo Archive.

The demolition of the Gorgie Road End at Tynecastle Stadium in 1997. The erection of the new stand meant the end of the 'free view' for the residents of the tenements behind.

Gary Mackay played a record number of games for Hearts. Behind him is the Wheatfield Stand. © Eric McCowat Sports Photo Archive.

Scunnered –Tosh McKinlay, Scott Crabbe, Walter Kidd, Derek Ferguson, George Wright and Gary Mackay at the Dinamo Bucharest Stadium in 1990.

John Robertson holding off Alan Sneddon and Gordon Hunter of Hibernian at Easter Road in March 1986. © Eric McCowat Sports Photo Archive.

Conditioning Derek Holmes' hamstrings on the new kit in the physiotherapy room at Tynecastle, 1996. Note the WWI stretcher behind the door.

A rare visit to the physiotherapy room from Pasquale Bruno.

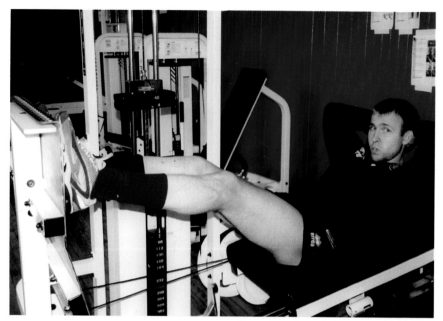

Slovakian internationalist Róbert Tomaschek, formerly of Slovan Bratislava, recovering from knee surgery in 2002.

Alan Rae flanked by Andy Kirk (left) and Scott Severin (right).

A rest day on the team's pre-season trip to Finland in 2002. The trio at the front are Stephen Simmons, Austin McCann and Andy Webster; behind them on the right are Stéphane Mahé, Scott Severin and Andy Kirk.

John Robertson being helped off the pitch in a match against Celtic by Alex MacDonald (left) and Alan Rae. © Eric McCowat Sports Photo Archive.

latter option and a sumptuous volley was dispatched into keeper Paddy Bonner's top left-hand corner. A point was gained from an unlikely quarter. For the Hearts fans, grief and pain were banished in an instant to be replaced by a frenzy of cheers, jumps, multiple raised fingers and the odd handstand from the 'Gulag' diehards.

As a therapist at a professional football club, I was always careful to remain in the background. There are many huge egos in pro soccer teams and Heart of Midlothian was no different. Sometimes, however, mixing with the public while accompanying the management was unavoidable.

I remember in 1994, after a pre-season match in Inverness, the team retired to Nairn where the players were allowed some free time. The twa Tams suggested we go for a light refreshment in a local hotel, nothing outrageous, just a couple of lagers, then bed.

Sitting quietly discussing the day's events, we were joined by three locals who seemed fairly sober and reasonable. They didn't sit down but stood at the table shooting the breeze. The lad behind me was stout and in his 40s. He casually placed my head and neck in an arm lock. This gradually tightened like a garrotte. I remained passive, trying not to create a public incident. Spots and flashing lights started to appear before my eyes. Meanwhile the others' conversation continued, interspersed with sips of lager. At the point when I was about to black out my executioner suddenly became bored and released me from the lock, whereupon I lifted my glass to appear cool and took a mouthful. It was a surreal experience and to this day I have no idea of what the guy was up to.

Hampden Park could never be called a home from home for the Jambos. Celtic Park was undergoing some serious rebuilding and Celtic was temporarily rehoused at the National Stadium. I had unfortunately witnessed eight Hearts visits there. Only once did they return with a victory. It is therefore easy to understand why a further visit in the league was regarded with some apprehension, especially since the Airdrieonians had seen us off earlier in the month on the same park in the cup semi-final. The fact that Celtic was the opposition reinforced the negativity. Points were precious as the season was drawing to a close but it was difficult to forecast where they would come from. Jim Bett had rescued a point, scoring from the spot on our last visit against Celtic. Would Tommy's team produce a shock? A triumph of hope over experience? Aye, right!

Along the way an ex-Rangers winger by the name of David Hagen had been taken on. He was a very solid lad for a winger, his backside would not have shamed Nijinsky, and I don't mean the ballet dancer. But he was seriously quick, and left-sided.

Under the lights at Hampden the tension grew. Neither side had scored as the game edged closer to the 90-minute mark. Often at this stage in matches against Celtic the roof would cave in. As Celtic continued the siege, watches were consulted nervously. Then a telling pass out of defence found David, unbelievably on his own, wide on the left. I knew right away that no one in a Hoops jersey could catch him. All he had in front of him were the goals and Paddy Bonner. How was he 'one on one' with the roly-poly? I needn't have worried. His finish was clinical – one-zip Hearts, a win against Celtic away from home and three precious points.

At the end of season 94–95 a scrutiny of the league table showed that, had Hearts lost or drawn that match, a play-off place to avoid relegation would have been inevitable.

Joe Jordan's time at the club had led to three seasons of stability but arguably his greatest contribution was the establishment of a youth policy. Having seen the direction the Old Firm was taking, he must have realised Hearts could not compete at that level of spending and so, with the board's approval, he committed more resources to the youth development programme at Tynecastle. Who said 'success has many fathers but failure is an orphan'? That tended to be what happened when Player X turned out to be a dud. When Alan McLaren, one of the few ball-playing centre halves ever to grace Tynecastle – and later Ibrox – emerged, there was no shortage of scouts coming forward claiming credit for his discovery.

It is largely because of Jordan and his network of scouts that players like Ritchie, McManus, Murie, Locke, Callaghan and Thomas emerged. On the strength of these lads the BP Youth Cup was won at Ibrox, no mean feat against a Rangers side which included Charlie Miller, an outstanding but wayward wing half.

Sandy Clark nurtured and coached all the youths through this period. He had been through the debacle at Croix, where that crop failed miserably (as described in Chapter 5), but now there were players progressing to the *first* team.

As manager in 1993 Sandy had taken the BP cup-winning squad (plus Allan Johnston, who was a year older than the rest) for an end of season U19 tournament near Chantilly. The venues were close to one of the locations for the Bond film *View to a Kill*. Hugh McCann and I had a walk round the race course and les Grandes Ecuries but never saw a horse.

Youth Tournaments in France and Germany are a big deal for the local community. Healthy crowds turn out, the sun shines, the smell of *pommes frites* and burgers is in the air, the local beer getting a hiding.

It all makes for a carnival atmosphere. Despite the distractions Hearts played well enough to reach the final against a very strong Le Havre side. When the game started a lanky player collected the ball in his own penalty box, set off through the left channel like a greyhound and on reaching the Hearts' box squared the ball to an onrushing team-mate. Bang: 1-0. The thought occurred to me that if he did that again we were in serious bother. Well, he didn't. The boys rolled up their sleeves and got mucked in to this bunch of 'posing bastards' (not my description of course). What a shift was put in. No more goals from Le Havre. With seconds to go centre back McManus got his head on the end of a cross ball to make it 1-1. After extra time it came down to penalties. Allan Johnston came up to take the clincher after the other lot had missed their fifth. He was buried under a heap of maroon bodies after scoring – never had I seen such a collective celebration of sheer joy.

What is worth mentioning about this squad was their behaviour. When the newspapers report on the outrageous antics of overpaid young footballers, I reflect on this group who were never a moment's bother off the park. That is not to say they were all Sunday school teachers but they respected Sandy, who had the ability and presence – physical and mental – to handle blossoming talent.

The decision to establish a comprehensive youth policy has been vindicated: today, some 20 years on, it appears to be stronger than ever with the net now being spread worldwide.

At the beginning of Sandy's time in charge the rumour had 'cascaded' (admin-speak) down the chain of command that Wallace Mercer was getting ready to offload the club, and clearly a Premier League team would be easier to move on than one from the First Division. Well, the orders were very clear: stay in the Premier. But how? There was a lot of debt and now Ian Baird had gone, who was going to partner Robbo? A foil for Hearts' leading scorer had been a problem since Sandy retired as a player. Could a player be found who fitted the bill without the bank hierarchy dissolving into hysterics?

The eventual decision was made after watching Justin Fashanu in a friendly match at Grangemouth in the summer of 1993. Here was a specimen-and-a-half. Just one look was enough to realise what an intimidating prospect he was likely to be for opposing defenders. Hearts have had a penchant for signing players who could manage a performance one game in three – that is, their sell-by date had been reached. Ali Mauchlen, David McCreery, Maurice Johnston, Vincent Guérin, Peter Marinello, to name but a few – all exceptional players at another time and another place. Justin was at this stage in his career.

He could still finish though. In training his performances at 'crossing and finishing' sessions were exemplary. Getting about the park was another story, as his right knee did not straighten fully. When I examined the joint, I quickly realised that physiotherapy would not shift it. All the structures round the knee had adapted to this loss of extendability; and when soft tissues become set in their ways in an adult, they can never be completely restored to their former state. How many surgeons had operated on or injected into this poor lad's joint? Hard to tell. I suspect that, as he was a £1 million player, everyone wanted a slice of the 'I cured Fashanu's knee!' action. Anyway, what Hearts saw was what they got and now we had to make the best of it.

We all knew he was gay – he came out publicly in 1990. John Robertson roomed with him regularly at away games or on tour. There was a lot of friendly team banter about wearing a long shirt or sleeping with his back to the wall. John never batted an eyelid.

A pre-season trip had been organised to northern Germany, where we were housed in a sports hotel in a small village called Wiefelstede. John Colquhoun met up with the squad there, moving back to the Jambos from Sunderland as Derek Ferguson went in the opposite direction. If JC could get the ball on to Fash's head, things might be looking up.

On this trip I was conned into driving a minibus to take the boys into Oldenburg for a night out. The deal was that Sandy would drive into town with half the squad then I would return to pick up the other half. I should have known better. Along the autobahn into downtown Oldenburg, first set of lights at red, everyone abandons ship, leaving me with the lights at green and in the passenger's seat! Traffic chaos, left-hand drive, wrong side of the road. Was it left or right or straight on? North to Wilhelmshaven, east to Bremen or south to Osnabruck? Did I have enough juice to get me back to the hotel if I bungled the directions? It only goes to show that socialising with players is inadvisable.

The remainder of the trip went well, although the rain was worse than anything I had experienced in the tropics. but the training pitches handled these downpours and were never unplayable. A fleet of bicycles were available at the hotel and races with Gary Locke through the flat countryside were welcome interludes between the twice daily training sessions.

By the time we returned from Germany a regimen of treatment had been worked out for Fash, most of it chemical. Having played at Nottingham Forest, a club which had won back-to-back European Cups, it was small wonder that he didn't hang around Tynecastle after training. For this 6 foot 4 swinger, Edinburgh beckoned.

Mornings are hectic for physiotherapists at a football club. Up to my neck one particular forenoon, I received a call. With my hands full and the phone wedged between neck and shoulder, I was informed that Mr Fashanu would be arriving at Haymarket Station on the 10.15 from Queen Street, and would I be sure to pick him up?

Firstly, I commuted by bike to Tynecastle, secondly cars were seldom available and thirdly, chauffeur I was not.

About 45 minutes later I was confronted by Justin in high dudgeon. Where had I been? Why didn't I obey the instructions? *And* did I know what it was like to be black and left standing at a strange railway station? The big blouse then stormed off. I followed him, suggesting that a taxi for a man of his means (he could afford a manservant) was surely the answer. Lateral thinking – not! But the air was cleared and there were no more requests for chauffeuring services.

CHAPTER 10

Canadian Capers

END OF SEASON trips from my point of view were largely done under sufferance – it was time away from my family and there was none of the hurly burly of competitive league football; but my job entailed duty of care to the players and when they were performing my presence was always necessary.

The trip to Canada in 1994, which took place over 20 years after the Hearts' previous visit, involved Celtic, Aberdeen and a side from Montreal. It was intended as a kind of fillip at the end of a trying season and an opportunity for team bonding on and off the park.

The three Scottish teams were on the same aircraft, which gave everyone a chance to forget the league and enjoy a bit of banter on the way across the Pond. On arrival we were taken to the suburban town of Hamilton, about half-an-hour's drive from Toronto. All three teams were to share the same billet.

Potential hazards are quickly noted in a new environment which you are about to share with young, testosterone-loaded athletes and this place certainly had its distractions. Across the street was a huge pizza take-away, which was fine, as hotel meals seldom satisfy footballers' appetites, but the concerning thing was that adjacent to it there was a lap-dancing bar. Terrific! Another block away, an Elvis impersonator in pink was warning people to stay 'offa his blue suede shoes' outside a massive amusement arcade. Sandy Clark was actually pleased about this setting – after all, this was not a pre-season trip, and within reasonable limits the players would certainly not be bored.

Celtic were an 'out of sorts' bunch. Lou Macari was in charge but there were two distinct staff camps: the old 'dyed-in-the-wool crew' such as Frank Connor, Neil Mochan and my colleague Brian Scott; then the manager and his squad of southerners. Not an easy relationship there, I thought.

After one training session Sandy spelt out the ground rules: 'Have a nice time but everyone back in their rooms by 11pm.' As football teams went, Hearts were a fairly restrained bunch with most of the lads being trusted. One ne'er do well needs someone to spark off – it takes two to tango – and I didn't see a pairing like that.

Maurice Johnston had been injury-free during his time at Tynecastle and for a lad who normally played with his stockings round his ankles, this was quite outstanding. However, he suddenly developed all sorts of aches and pains and my notion of a few clinic-free days went out the window as his treatment became a daily ritual.

A story about Mo and his colourful lifestyle when he was at Rangers had come my way: allegedly, when on tour with the Teddies, he was told to disappear for a few days and turn up at the designated departure time in order to catch the plane home. I mentioned this to Sandy, thinking he might treat him in a similar fashion, but the manager was having none of it.

While the sun shone everything was fine but when the wind changed and blew off Lake Ontario it was much the same as a wet weekend in Airdrie. The matches we played were at an all-weather American Football stadium. The surface, although green in colour, did not absorb the intense heat, instead reflecting it, thus turning the stadium into a cauldron. The Quebec team the Jambos were to face was managed by former Charlton Athletic player Eddie Firmani, whose picture I had last seen as a schoolboy collecting football photos given away with a brand of bubble gum. Here was a man who had played in Italy at the highest level, a striker who had scored prolifically wherever he went, particularly for Charlton.

At the peak of his career in Italy, Firmani would have been earning the equivalent of what the average Premier League player is paid now. I asked myself what was he doing here, managing a team called Montreal Impact (if I recall correctly), in a country which has nine months of winter. The game itself was memorable for me as I saw Mo

Healthy eating – not! Alan McLaren, Les Porteous and Paul Ritchie, Toronto, 1994.

sorting out a couple of French Canadians when the game got a little tousy.

Football always makes for strange bedfellows and on this trip we were looked after by some pretty shady-looking ex-pats. These guys were as nice as pie. One of them, our 'courier', was a convert to baseball and he'd even soldered the team badges onto his cap; the winters are, after all, long in Canada. There had to be a sting and it came in the shape of tickets for what to me was a glorified game of rounders. The local Blue Jays (back-to-back World Series Champions, we were told, but where were the Chinese, Russian, or German teams in this 'world league'?) were playing the Cleveland Indians. The stadium was magnificent and, if you were daft enough, you could walk all around the inside and spend three times your ticket money on junk! Our 30-dollar seats were behind the pitcher, well behind – about 300 metres. The Blue Jays' top man, Joe Carter, won the match with a home run from the last pitch of the day, just in time to see the last coat of paint drying. As underwhelming experiences go, this was right up there. The

Pilmar Smith, Les Porteous, Hugh McCann and Sandy Clark in Toronto, outside the Blue
Jays' stadium, Toronto, 1994.

day was saved when we spotted Alan McLaren disappearing into his
room with a pizza the size of a painter's pasting table!

Tourist attractions in this neck of Canada were mostly man-made
– tall buildings and strange architectural follies which tourists could
ascend to see more of a pretty boring landscape. However there was
a waterfall of some note about an hour's drive away, a trip surely not
to be missed. Most of us took the chance of a boat trip which ferried
groups as close as we would have cared to go to the edge of Niagara

Falls. We all wore blue polythene waterproofs, which made us look like giant condoms. Attractions like this have to have sideshows and instead of the boat trip, on the advice and leadership of Mo, three or four of the party opted for the ghost train, the dodgems and candy floss.

On returning to Hamilton we found that the hotel was hosting the event of the year, a Gay Motorcycle Festival. The place was crowded with young men in very tight leather gear, Ray-Bans and kit associated with the young Marlon Brando in *The Wild One*. It occurred to me that getting out of the lift on the wrong floor could be problematic, as goalie Henry Smith and Hoggie were to find out. As I was to learn later, on another trip to Canada, all sorts of waifs and strays arrive at events like this to take the opportunity of meeting exotic strangers, including randy footballers. After a few beers both Henry and Hoggie were heading for their respective kips but contrived to get in the wrong bedrooms. They soon found out the error of their ways as they gate-crashed some interesting parties and sharp exits were made by both.

The return trip was thankfully uneventful, the calm before the storms of take-over and change of management.

It was to be another ten years before Hearts visited Canada again and when they did it was expressly business. Three managers had come and gone and Craig Levein was now at the helm. He had signed up-and-coming young men who had a streak of individuality about them, but blending the likes of Patrick Kisnorbo, Kevin McKenna, Alan Maybury and Paul Hartley and the 'bonus ball', Neil MacFarlane, into a team was a big ask.

Neil was a jewel. Having somehow slipped under the radar of the big clubs, he had played for a Glasgow amateur team until he was 20. A serious knee injury which had arrested his progress through the professional ranks had been repaired but his current team could not afford the cost of rehabilitation. Somewhere prior to his injury, Craig had seen Neil and felt he could do a job in the top flight if he was sound and fit. After assessing the lad I felt it would depend on his attitude to the rehab process rather than anything this programme contained. I needn't have worried. Neil, who was a natural in all games including snooker, tennis and golf, worked his socks off, day in and day out, with the reward a run in the first team and a chance to participate in a European competition.

I did not know it at the time of leaving for Vancouver but there was another new signing who would cause me some exasperation. His name was Ramon Perreira, a Spanish lad who sported the worst mullet I'd seen in years. Like another Iberian, Nacho Novo, he had enjoyed a spell with Raith Rovers in the Kingdom of Fife. Craig, as we know, enjoyed a punt in the transfer market but this looked like an ante-post outsider (ante-post: placing a bet on a horse weeks before its race in order to get better odds).

Vancouver is either the northern gateway to the east or the east's sneaky way into the west and it boasts an incredible mix of nationalities. The city centre, with its close proximity to the water ringed by steep hills, made me think of Hong Kong. Unlike our humble Hamilton abode, the hotel was modern and the cuisine excellent, with meals laid on buffet-style to allow the players to get enough to eat without resorting to 'grazing' in shopping centres.

The club had extended itself in employing a sports masseur after coach Bert Logan left. Bert's book-making business was entering the era of the internet, which probably meant more work for him and less time to devote to the Hearts, which he had given freely. David Valentine, Bert's successor, was a professional musician and good with his hands. As a younger man he had been a successful runner, particularly at the New Year professional meet. Adaptable and versatile, he had won over four distances – 90, 110, 400 and 800 metres – something he brings up from time to time, particularly when I mention my own attempts at middle distance. We also share the same chronic disorder – an obsession with fishing, not that the fish need worry as we are both pretty duff!

The heat in training was overpowering and the fair-haired guys like Stampy and McKechnie (this was what McKenna was called by his team-mates) wore floppy cricket hats throughout. With temperatures hovering around the 100 degrees fahrenheit mark, it was unlikely that there would be any pulled muscles but one player who was never going to over-train was Ramon. Once again here was a player with an obscure injury, nothing to see or feel, full range of movement and a negative report on the X-ray.

Soft tissue injuries are not in the same league as problems with the central nervous or cardio-vascular systems. The guidelines are pain, swelling, redness, local heat and loss of function. If these are not observed then the notion that this might be a problem of psychogenic origin arises. Trust me, it is better for player and therapist that this remains 'a notion'. Feedback from the musculoskeletal system to the brain may indeed be negative, presenting the player with an incomplete picture of how that area is functioning and it would be poor practice to ignore this.

Ramon had a lot going on and he was never off the phone to his girlfriend or mother but his command of English did not extend to explaining his affairs of the heart. Football needs 'willing horses' and at this time Ramon couldn't raise a gallop. He wasn't a bad lad though. With the benefit of hindsight, I feel he may have been chronically homesick during his time with the Jambos.

After our return from Canada I was to become well acquainted with him. Often we would talk about bull fighting, something he knew a lot about, whereas my knowledge extended to the bull always being 6/4 against. One day in mid-season he appeared in the physio's room at Tynie with a stack of videos under his arm. Here was the complete history of the bullring, from the Corrida to the Veronica. Over a couple of weeks I did justice to the films and in one clip I caught a glimpse of the statue of Sir Alexander Fleming outside the Plaza de Toros de Las Ventas in Madrid. Grateful matadors had raised the cash to honour this man from Darvel, whose discovery of penicillin had saved the lives of many who, after being gored, would otherwise have died of septicaemia.

Word had got around Vancouver that 20 or so professional ball players had arrived to train and play a few matches. 'Working girls' started to appear at the hotel, taking over the cocktail bar adjacent to the restaurant, where they could size up the talent and potential customers. This ploy must have failed as they resorted to displaying their wares around the swimming pool, which was overlooked by the players' rooms. This exhibition was at least 'live' and probably more diverting than the pay-per-view channels, which normally took a battering from young men who had to endure ten days of celibacy.

The training went well in Vancouver. Millwall FC were in the same location and due to play the Jambos on the Saturday afternoon, when the sun was at its hottest. Ray Wilkins, a man of many top clubs, including Manchester United, Rangers and, dare I say it, Hibernian, was in charge of Millwall. Derek Ferguson has described him as the 'nicest man in the wurrald!' Actually, he *was* OK. But why wasn't the kick-off later in the day? Very often, thinking and planning don't go together in football and on this occasion, as a result, the public got a less than an energetic performance and it took two days for the teams to recover.

A young Andrew Driver made his debut for the first team on the west coast of Canada, although within ten minutes of his big day he had removed himself to the side of the park and brought up his stomach contents! It might have been a touch of the sun or something he couldn't digest but regardless of the cause, the thought of a pleasant boat trip to our next game on Victoria Island couldn't have been further from his mind.

The night before this match was spent in a Country and Western-style motel; it was at times like these that I would think: 'What am I doing here?'

Canadian-born Kevin McKenna, the Hearts centre back, put in a great performance, scoring a hat-trick against a local Select XI, probably for the benefit of his parents, who attended the match. Ramon remained a spectator throughout the tour, which must have established a club record for a player to travel so far without stripping, so no doubt he was relieved to be boarding the plane home.

Team spirit, bonding and playing for your mates are all usually enhanced by living and socialising together and this was broadly seen as being the case with these two trips to Canada. But, as with the Romanian trip described earlier, things don't always pan out as planned.

CHAPTER 11
Italian Renaissance

WHEN JIM JEFFERIES rolled into Tynecastle as manager in 1995, it didn't take him long to determine that the squad he had inherited was in need of a major overhaul. He and his assistant Billy Brown were the first professionals ever to ask me for my assessment of the squad. My response: 'No legs!'

There were some decent youngsters but they needed time and guidance and Craig Levein's knee problem would keep him out of action for some time. With the defence leaking goals, Jim knew a transfusion of fresh blood was required – enter the imposing figure of Pasquale Bruno. My first encounter with this Italian athlete was in a hotel in Corstorphine just after he had arrived in Edinburgh. Wow! Dress him in a Crombie coat, put a snap brim hat on his head and you had a character straight out of Mario Puzo's *The Godfather*. I had a vision of Pasquale entering the dressing room at half time, looking towards the gaffer and saying: 'Ally McCoist sleeps with the fishes...'

A thorough professional who paid great attention to detail, Pasquale was immaculate on and off the park. Once the action got under way he was also ruthless, a trait which would serve the team well as he set about dragging Hearts away from the relegation zone. A reputation for bad behaviour was not long in arriving, but so what, if he could inspire an ailing Hearts side to safety? There was also a compassionate side to his nature, something I appreciated when he was one of the first to offer his condolences after my mother died.

Purely from a physiotherapist's perspective he was a delight to work with – he never had an injury, at least he never declared one, and was always available for selection.

Pasquale was another player for whom the move to Hearts represented a huge culture shock, not least the changing facilities after training at Musselburgh. Here was a player from the highest level of the game in Europe now having to change in a local leisure centre. Any discomfort he may have felt at his new surroundings would surely have eased somewhat when he looked at his bank statement. The club took great care of him. Installed at the Caledonian Hotel on Princes Street he would say to our bus driver Allan Scott: 'All-an, putta me oaf at my 'ouse.'

As with any high-profile signing, the benefits can be felt off as well as on the pitch. For the Hearts, spin-offs from Pasquale's arrival were many. The press loved the chemistry surrounding him and the reporters were always waiting for the match when he would 'chin' somebody. A few team-mates were a bit slower to warm to him, in fact the whiff of resentment was noticeable until he won them over with his quality and sheer professionalism as an athlete. I am sure that the youngsters of that era took forward long into their careers what Pasquale left them with.

The ground staff found 'Pasquale' a bit of a mouthful, so he got 'Bruno' from them, which he didn't seem to resent. He was a character in every sense of the word. Jefferies recalled with a laugh the occasion he was about to give him his instructions before the return leg of a European tie: 'Quick as a flash he said, "I know gaffer, you want your best player to mark their best player!"' Pasquale was not unaware of his pedigree but generally he wasn't one to make a big deal out of it.

Bobby Clyde, a young man on Hearts' books at the time, was assigned to clean his boots, put out his kit and generally act as his valet. He recalls that on the day of his debut, just to make his mark, Pasquale moved his jersey to where he wanted it to be in the dressing room. Medium-size shorts were demanded, as he did not want to 'looka like a clown ina baggy pants'.

One day Pasquale asked if he could get three of his own shirts laundered professionally. In the winter the club was in the habit of using the local launderette for the kit the in-house plant couldn't handle. Off went Bobby with the shirts. On the day of their expected

Jim Jefferies relaxing after his first season in charge.

return, Pasquale was at the club in the early afternoon to discuss some contractual details. Immaculate as ever, in sand-coloured slacks, blue shirt, navy jacket and brown moccasins, he collared Bobby: 'You go pick up my shirts, Boabee!' The attendant stated that there had only ever been two. Pasquale was duly informed. The blue touch-paper had been lit. He returned with Bobby to confront the launderette staff: 'Wherea my shairt – you steal it for a your 'usband? You need money? I geeve you money?' Well, diplomacy in Gorgie Road is an alien concept and there was no chance of any conciliatory gestures coming from behind the counter. 'Fuck off back to Italy you tally bastard!' came the retort. Pasquale advanced further only to be restrained and then huckled to the door by his boot boy. He straightened his jacket, shook himself down and returned to the club. The story got better and better as the season progressed just as the cries of 'Bruno – Bruno!' increased from the terraces.

Before one European tie, Bobby asked him if he was nervous about his marking role. 'Nervos? Nervos? When you 'ave marked Maradona,

Van Basten and Carreca... oo ees thees guy you talk about? *Ee ees nervos!*'

It would take a considerable event to faze a man like this but events at Ibrox one Saturday in January '96 showed that he could be stirred by happenings on the park.

The team was gradually being transformed into one that could again be something of a force in Scotland. Allan Johnston, who came to the fore that year and was now a first team regular along with Gary Locke, was probably the lightest player I had ever weighed when he was taken on – under 50 kilos – less than a hundredweight in 'old money'. Keeping the ball up, he could jog around Tynecastle without it once touching the ground.

Hearts had opened the scoring, Allan getting on the end of some great wing work by John Colquhoun to stun the home fans. Just before half time things got even better when he added a second. During the second half Pasquale was taken off to be replaced by Gary Mackay. When Allan placed his third past the stranded Andy Goram, Pasquale could be heard to intone as he leaned against the wall of the dug-out: 'Hunbelievable, hunbelievable, hunbelievable.' Clearly the man was touched.

One of the last games Pasquale played for Hearts was at the junior ground in Musselburgh, Olivebank. He certainly made an impression with the visitors, a Raith Rovers eleven. An opposing striker was being a bit naughty with one of the Hearts centre backs, so at a corner kick the marking was changed. The ball was cleared but a forward was on the ground nursing a sore nose. The experience of Seria A had surfaced.

By the time Hearts won the cup, Pasquale had left the club. During the post-match celebrations in the Gorgie Suite he appeared and his reception was every bit as tumultuous as that accorded earlier to the triumphant team. Did he milk the occasion? Just a little! After all, he truly was a star.

A friendly against Hamilton Academicals on a Heriot-Watt playing field was the unlikely venue for a rare African talent to come to the attention of the Jefferies' coaching team. A little guy with flowing dreadlocks stole the show with a virtuoso performance. Nobody could get near him when he had the ball. Great balance with pace to go with it – how did *this* end up in Scotland? His name was José Manuel Quitongo, with the 'J' pronounced as a 'J', not 'H'. An Angolan from Luanda, he credited his astonishing pace to his time in the bush escaping lions! He was a real character and certainly lit up the dressing room at Tynecastle when he came to Hearts in 1997.

Our kit manager Norrie had some real verbal skirmishes with José, all good-natured. José was always on the tap, looking for freebies for his family in Hamilton, or so he said. He had more tricks up his sleeve than Chan Canasta. When a request for kit was knocked back by Norrie, his riposte was loud and clear: '*Norrie, you rassist!*'

Flights were never dull when José was on board. A clever mimic, his favourite hoax was to meow when storing his hand luggage. Stewardesses regularly fell for it and scuttled up and down the aisle searching for this non-existent moggie. When they discovered the truth, they seemed to find it impossible to be angry with this little charmer. It would be wrong of me to state that he was sure to be a member of the Mile High Club but Hearts defender Grant (Bert) Murray summed him up by saying: 'He'd get a piece at onybuddy's door!'

Watching him play at Tynecastle one Saturday I noted that José often beat the same player more than once during the same attack. This trick which reminded me of a time when Bobby Parker was on the Hearts board and told me about an incident in a reserve game at Ibrox against Rangers as he was nearing the end of his playing career. An up-and-coming Davie Wilson was on the left wing for Rangers. Bobby, at right back, was no match for this fast forward who would go on to play for Scotland and help to end the Hampden hoodoo when Scotland beat the Auld Enemy 2-0 on a sunny Saturday afternoon in April 1962.

Wilson had taken the ball up to Bobby and beat him but instead of passing or delivering the ball, he allowed Bobby to get back to have another bite at it, in order to 'do' him again. This was happening too often, a senior pro was being taken to the cleaners and humiliation was not to be tolerated. During a lull in play, Bobby told the disrespectful winger to pass or deliver but not 'take the piss'. The warning went unheeded and Wilson was to feel the wrath of his brassed-off opponent when Rangers won a corner. As all eyes waited for the incoming ball, Wilson's 'tackle' was seized and squeezed, with a wrench thrown in for good measure. The ball was cleared down field when a crumpled heap in blue-and-white was noticed writhing in the six-yard box clasping his mangled manhood.

With this tale in mind I wondered how long it would take before an exasperated defender would mete out the same treatment to José but it never happened. José was just too fly!

CHAPTER 12
Norrie Gray

DUE TO THE SIZE of the squad and a burgeoning youth policy it was becoming clear that coaches and physiotherapists had their hands full without having to prepare and deliver nicely folded kit. On our return from a pre-season trip to Dublin, it was discovered that a bag of kit had been left behind at the hotel, which relieved me of the burden of being left to deal with that side of things.

After two seasons in charge, Jefferies and Brown found sympathetic ears in Robinson and Deans when they set out their case for bringing in a new member of the backroom team. Training areas at Pinkie Primary School in Musselburgh and at Levenshall had been acquired, due in no small part to Billy's local knowledge and connections. Changing facilities were either at Olivebank or the sports centre near Inveresk. As a result there were logistical problems regarding the delivery of kit.

A man well known to the management team was approached to bring order from chaos. This was Norrie Gray, a telecom engineer who had a knowledge of sports injuries, having attended courses run by Tom McNiven for the Scottish FA. Norrie had a wealth of experience of football in the east of Scotland, having worked for three junior sides and two senior outfits, one of which was Berwick Rangers, where he had met Jim Jefferies. As kit manager, Norrie's main asset to Hearts was his ability to organise. Away from football, most coaches and managers would have difficulty finding a loaf in a bakery but as a former matelot, Norrie had been disciplined into neatness. Aboard ship every item had its place and had to fit, no square pegs in round holes, Mr Starbuck!

Although fixture schedules could be hectic, having Norrie in post meant that the management could relax and coaches could coach without any concern about players being inadequately turned out. And the physio had met someone whom he could trust implicitly.

Before the move to Heriot-Watt University at Riccarton, the youth players – our ground staff – had duties which were rotated in order that the less pleasant tasks were shared out. Nobody wanted to be the latrine wallah for a season, whereas caring for the management's kit was undemanding.

These lads soon learned that sloppy work would no longer be tolerated. Norrie's 'It's my way, son, OR AGAIN!' was soon hard-wired into their grey matter. A 'two bucket floor' was precisely that. If anyone was caught washing a dressing room floor without a change of water halfway through, it would then become a 'four bucket floor'.

It must be remembered that a descent into anarchy was only a few bad results away. Relegation would almost certainly return the Jambos to the situation of the early 1980s, so ensuring that professionalism extended from top to bottom was key and was one of the factors which kept the club in the top flight.

Youngsters joining the ground staff often had little notion of the world outside of football. Two recent signings deployed to laundry duties were nicknamed 'Sickboy' and 'Sea-Bass' by their more senior team-mates. One of them did have a passing resemblance to a character in Trainspotting, but 'Sea-Bass' had me stumped.

With my background in health services I had developed a keen sense of smell honed to recognising odours which did not fit the circumstances in which they were hovering. One morning while applying a strapping to an ankle, I caught a whiff of serious body odour. The player was wearing a very niffy T-shirt, and he was not alone. The problem? A discriminating Sickboy had been turning certain items round very quickly, taking the view that if the shirts were not visibly soiled they could just be dried. The error of his ways was soon pointed out to Mr Neilson and we all began to breathe more easily.

Sea-Bass was instructed that the last item to go in the wash would be the whites, which went through a very hot wash. He did put the items in last – but with the maroon T-shirts! This resulted in pink knickers for the players, gay blades or not. Did the boy learn? Not until after this was repeated with a blue result, were less exacting duties found for this big fish.

A full-time kit manager was a great advance for the club and when it came to foreign players arriving, it was usually Norrie who sorted out their problems. As I found out on my travels, trying to understand a local French patois was way beyond what I had been taught at school. And so I sympathised with Gilles Rousset when he told me that sitting in the Falkirk dressing room on his debut, every second word he heard was 'fuck'. Managers in full flow at half time also show little consideration for non-nationals. I expect that most of them had heard tirades before, albeit in a different tongue: 'Get yer blankety blank finger oot o' yer blankety blank chapter and verse' is universal.

Management had chosen well from the foreign market. Rousset, Flögel, Adam and Salvatore were all top pros. Norrie was quick to recognise when all was not well with them and he was adept at negotiating their idiosyncracies.

When resting, Gilles (the big chap did get the odd day off from full training), was undemanding. 'Norree, I want a bath avec beaucoup bubbels, a black coffee… and a blow job! *Merci.*' The first two requests were easily delivered, who supplied the third is a mystery to all but the recipient.

Stefano Salvatore, who joined the club on Pasquale's recommendation, had an upper thigh problem. It is not unusual for new signings to sustain injuries early in their stay as they adapt to different training methods in new surroundings, making the acquaintance of Irn-Bru, haggis suppers, deep fried Mars Bars, etc.

It can take a lot out of a player having to cope with psycho-social factors. When it was explained to Stefano that a minor operation was required, Norrie and I expected it would be back to Italy to have this repair carried out. Not so. Unlike many foreign big hitters, he was content to have the procedure performed locally. So it was, and the operation was successful – phew!

Our foreign team members used Norrie as a conduit to other backroom staff and as a fount of local knowledge, such as where to find the best butcher, where to get fresh pasta, TV repairs and the like. All simple enough requests but to a stranger in town, particularly one with a young family in tow, potentially stressful. Finding the closest general practice willing to take on the family was often the problem. When a child is involved, you or I would accept the GP's advice that 'It's just a wee cold, give them hot drinks, keep them warm and all will be well in 72 hours.' Alas, that would not satisfy highly paid footballers, so either Norrie or I would take the family off to the 'Sick Kids' hospital and explain that the family have no English but need some reassurance regarding the bairn's snottery nose!

It was Norrie's contention that the top players' needs were always minimal. Others not in the top flight could be, and often were, more difficult to satisfy. Increased kit availability allowed players to become more picky and idiosyncratic. 'Ah cannae gie ye whut ah huvnae gote' no longer applied.

The amount of kit carried to away games in the '80s had quadrupled by the affluent '90s, and the days of vice chairmen having to raid Marks & Spencers for players' briefs prior to matches were well and truly gone. Before I left the club, six hampers of kit were loaded on the bus for away matches!

Three sets of jerseys, (two sets long sleeved, one set short sleeved), 32 pairs of shorts, two full sets of stockings, two full sets of briefs – and this was only the match gear. Warm-up T-shirts, match T-shirts, sweat tops, waterproofs and jogging bottoms, then the specialist goalkeeping clothing – don't forget, the roly-poly can touch the ball with every part of his anatomy – boots, 'leathers' and 'mouldies', extra studs, pliers, laces, boot brushes and polish would just about cover it.

I am reliably informed that some players now have up to six pairs of boots packed. (Changed days indeed. Gary Mackay wore a pair of Adidas 'Montevideo' for years. At the finish there were more patches on them than original boot leather. A rumour or not I don't know, but I did hear that when Dick Advocaat was in charge at Ibrox he made the players responsible for their own boots.)

Then there are warm-up balls, bibs and cones and tactics boards. In winter, hats and gloves. Where will it all end? My equipment and the

Thomas Flögel gets a 'nose job' from the physio. Photograph © Scotsman Publications Ltd.

medical cases were always checked the night before with the ice packs made up on the morning prior to leaving for the match. Any omissions could be embarrassing.

Brian Whittaker travelled to an Aberdeen reserve fixture without the match boots, while on another occasion in the Granite City, Teddy Scott had to supply us with shin pads. On a pre-season trip to Germany, no match shorts provided another hurdle to overcome. Small items indeed, but 'for the want of a shoe, the battle was lost'.

Players are creatures of habit and preserving their mental equilibrium is an essential part of preparation. The other aspect, of course, is how mistakes reflect on the club.

Alan Rae with kit manager Norrie Gray at Gullane for a pre-season training session.

On the morning of the 1998 cup final, Norrie and two ground staff travelled with the match kit to Parkhead, where Hearts had been allocated the home dressing room. This may have been a fiddle to keep the Teddies from misbehaving, but I think that it is normally the toss of a coin which decides such things. At semi-finals it is the team first out of the hat.

While he was engrossed in his painstaking tasks he was visited by a pride of Lisbon Lions – Steve Chalmers, Bertie Auld, Bobbie Lennox, Ronnie Simpson and Norrie's counterpart, John Clark – who to a man said: 'You're no gonnae let that lot win the cup here of all places.' The undercurrents of a Rangers victory would cut the Parkhead faithful to the bone.

The triumphant events of that May afternoon are recorded elsewhere but as a result of post-match drug tests, the return of the team to Edinburgh was delayed – players are so dehydrated after a game that it takes approximately an hour-and-a-half, sometimes longer, for players to produce a urine sample.

In the chaos which followed at Tynecastle, the hampers were left outside the dressing room, unlocked. The next morning the kit had vanished! The jerseys did, however, turn up in the most unusual place. At the 1998 World Cup finals in the Stade de France, while watching the opening match, Brazil v Scotland, Norrie spotted them being worn by spectators who lived not a thousand miles from Bonnyrigg!

With the move to the training centre at Heriot-Watt University in 2004, Norrie's post assumed more importance. Living cheek by jowl with the uni staff meant increased discipline for the players – and no more urinating on the rose bushes.

It will be some time before the effects of a move to a place outside of the recognised football establishment can be assessed. The training facilities at Heriot-Watt are certainly a hundred times better than anything Hearts had before, but I think that the future might be to follow the model of leading European sides like Bayern Munich and Inter Milan and rent a top class ground with good infrastructure. Oh, hold on... a pig just flew past the window.

CHAPTER 13

War Horses

AS WE ALL KNOW, football is a game of skill and artistry, but allied to these components are strength and resolution. The players who are relied upon to be strong and determined are just as important to the team effort as the gifted artists; the latter can, for a variety of reasons, including temperament, become Peter Bradys and disappear from the action, along with their contribution to the team effort. Individual battles have to be won all over the park for the team to be victorious.

I was browsing in a book shop when I came across Alistair Moffat's tome on the Border Reivers, which contains an off-piste paragraph describing the Battle of Tours, where Charles Martel's army 'saw off' the invading Muslims. Moffat maintains that Martel's heavy cavalry was too much for the lighter Arabian horses which were just battered from the field, prompting the end of the Islamic advance in Europe. There are parallels in team sports, as you may agree after reading the following.

'Getting good ball' in rugby is what the backs thrive on; for this they depend on the 'heavy mob' – the forwards. When Neil Lennon was a player at Parkhead, he was apparently told by Martin O'Neill: 'Cover the ground, win the ball, then give it to someone who can use it.' Hearts had players who could do this and it is not my intention to imply that they were any the less skilful than their comrades. Walter Kidd and Neil Berry played on the same side of the park. Anyone who watched the team in their era will appreciate how their efforts allowed JR, Gary Mackay and JC to flourish. Walter and Neil 'suffered for their art'. Turning in the glaur at Brockville, Walter wrecked his knee. At the Royal Infirmary 24 hours later, Master Surgeon Macnicol pushed a large bore needle into the joint to draw off a quarter pint of blood and there followed a six-month rehabilitation struggle. Broken hands, loss of sight, ankle and foot ligament tears were all in Papa's cv. (The supporters called him Zico but to the younger players he was Papa, just as John Cumming was Faither to the Hearts team of the '50s.) How often the night before a match against the Jambos did Peter Weir, Joe McBride and the late Davie Cooper – Aberdeen, Hibernian and Rangers left wingers respectively – lie awake thinking about what awaited them when they took the ball down the left wing at Tynie?

Neil Berry had his fair share of muscle and joint injuries and, like Walter, he damaged an eye. It was his attitude to the recovery process that saw him through. Even when out of favour he plugged away in the reserves, not an easy task for a first team player used to the hype of big match days. Even after a year out with a cruciate injury, Neil still played in over 300 games at Hearts.

Justice was done to these honest lads. Walter received a testimonial on a wet Sunday following a defeat the previous day by our neighbours, in spite of which a healthy crowd turned up to pay their respects. Before the match the professional sprinter Roy Heron ran an exhibition race which added some spice to the occasion. A few years later Olympic Lyonnais, a top class team, came over for Neil's match. Neil's testimonial strip, a sort of pink tartan, ranked highly in the 'howler' category, but Neil didn't have to wear it for very long as he was concussed early in the first half and removed from the field of play. He didn't see much after that, missing a solitary Allan Johnston goal.

Having a diminutive striker leading the line caused the Hearts management some concern. Willie Pettigrew had faded from the scene along with Derek O'Connor, the latter having partnered JR briefly. Jimmy Bone was durable but on the wrong side of 30. With Alex and Sandy handling this seasoned professional with care, often leaving him to do his running on a Saturday, he was rarely injured. It has to be said, though, that his shape at that stage of his career excluded him from the rigours of Alex's training.

When Jimmy moved on to management elsewhere, Alex pulled off a master-stroke by signing a Rangers striker who was out of favour in Govan. Sandy Clark had arrived at Ibrox from Airdrie via a stop-over at West Ham United. He had 'muscled up' since his earlier days at Broomfield and his ability to shield the ball and retain possession was no doubt welcomed by the defence behind him.

When the ball is played up to forwards and is sent back by return of post, the back line is soon under the cosh, against the collar, or just plain puffed out, whatever cliché you want. To relieve this situation, forwards have to keep the ball. Enter Clarky – this was where he excelled. I don't know how many forwards benefited from his coaching and advice on this particular aspect of forward play, but few could match him. His other attributes were durability, strength and a great touch, while from my point of view, he remained amazingly injury free. With a wee striker sniffing around his duels with opposing centre halves, this partnership promised to bear fruit for the Jambos.

On a very cold day in 1986 with the Tynecastle pitch frozen but flat, Hearts took on Rangers in the Scottish Cup. Challenges and tackles with the park in this condition look and sound more bone-jarring than normal and Clarky often found himself in the middle of the action regardless of conditions.

Following an aerial clash, he and Craig Paterson both ended flat on the icy pitch with head wounds. The frontal wound Clarky sustained was as bad as I have ever witnessed. His forehead was gaping with a huge laceration, the damage spreading in three directions, which meant there were two headaches in the treatment room – one Clarky's, the other Doc Melvin's, who wondered how he would sew this mess together. Of course the warrior wanted to continue but as a player with an outstanding ability to head the ball, this wound would be vulnerable to further damage and possible infection.

The two hardy lads from that time, Kidd and Clark, were great buddies who roomed together on away trips. Walter was often the subject of ribbings from his room-mate for carrying an iron with him to ensure that his clothes were just 'so'. He was fastidious, no doubt about it.

After Jim Jefferies' first season the squad, including me, went to a Spanish resort to spend a few days in the sun. For one reason or another I hadn't packed adequately and was looking like a 'paraffin lamp', whereas Walter was attired magnificently. One evening we went down for dinner, Walter had pushed the boat out: tropical silk shirt, matching shorts (pressed, of course) and a tan belt which matched his sandals saw him present himself in immaculate fashion. At the door of the dining room, Jim, Billy, Bert and I (the tramp) walked through. Walter was stopped by the maître d': 'Sorry, Sair, no shorts allowed in the dining area.' Did we have a wee snigger? You bet!

A successful signing who just fits into the war horse category was Steven Pressley. This was a real coup for Jim Jefferies as Steven was playing successfully with Dundee United where, according to Archie Knox (former assistant manager to Sir Alex Ferguson and Walter Smith), he had benefited from the defensive coaching of Maurice Malpas. In Pressley Hearts were fortunate in acquiring a centre back who had his youthful, erratic years behind him. He was to become the main man in the centre of an ever-changing Hearts defence. Having watched every game in which Steven played up to 2005, I was constantly impressed at how he imposed himself on taller and often stronger forwards. Most football players add an inch or so to their height when asked how tall they are but I don't think Steven ever did. At a stretch he maybe got to six feet; first thing in the morning – six one. He could not be described as 'towering' but his timing of defensive headers made up for his relative lack of height.

One of Steven's specialities was earning free kicks for his team. It was normal for forwards of any hue to fall in the box when rash contact was made from an opposition defender. Steven reversed this: when he fell in his own box it was to relieve pressure on the Hearts defence. For example, if there was a build up of opposition pressure and Steven was in possession of the ball, rather than clearing it blindly or putting it in row Z, he would invite a tackle from a forward. Now this skill – tackling – is not a forte of strikers, so when Steven was between the forward and the ball the slightest untoward 'touch' would see Steven go to ground. The ensuing free kick allowed the team to get up the park or to threaten the opposition penalty area. Some may cry it's cheating but it just depends which side you are on!

Steven 'Elvis' Pressley in the physio room at Tynecastle.

One Saturday when Kilmarnock was the opposition, Steven had pulled this stroke a couple of times, much to the frustration of Jefferies and Brown (who were in charge of Killie at the time). The dugouts are quite close together at Tynie so when Steven got away with it a third time an incensed Billy Brown roared across to anyone on the Hearts bench who would listen: 'That's fucking awful, he shouldnae be allowed tae dae that!' I thought that a bit rich, considering JJ and BB brought him to the club when he was still impressionable and had no doubt played a big part in his education.

When Gordan Petric came to Hearts, he most certainly fitted the 'tough laddie' description. Here was a naturally strong man who would grab unfortunate team-mates with one hand between the neck and the shoulder in what he called a 'death grip', a Balkan method of bonding, no doubt. One squeeze from this mighty hand and the writhing recipient was laid flat out.

We did have a bit of fun with Gordan as I could see that Steven, often one of his victims, would be up for a bit of leg pulling. Playing a European tie against Stuttgart in the Gottlieb Daimler Stadion,

Hearts were striving to keep the score at 1-0 which, against an average Bundesliga team, would not be an insurmountable hurdle to clear in the Tynecastle return leg. With about 20 minutes to go, Gordan sustained a small nick on his lower brow. It wasn't serious enough to stitch but it bled profusely, as head and facial wounds do. We put him back on the pitch with a small dressing to cover the wound, as anything larger would have interfered with his vision and with the minutes ticking away and the pressure mounting, Hearts needed his presence.

So what did the big eejit do? Every spare minute he had a poke at the dressing, which eventually came off, drawing the ref's attention to the flow of blood. Doc Steyn (standing in for Doc Melvin) and I were exasperated as he was led to the side for further attention – could the big goat 'no tak a tellin'? In the next couple of minutes though, the phrase 'Lion of Stuttgart' was coined as we pushed him back on the park with another dressing in place. There was no further score and as we walked back to the dressing room Gordan's performance was deemed to be leonine, particularly when the size of the cut was revealed to less than sympathetic team-mates, especially Mr Pressley. 'No munny folk wud huv played oan wi' that size o' cut, it must bae at least half an inch!'

Before and after Gary Naysmith, Hearts' home-grown international full back, Hearts signed two lads who were formidable defenders. The first was Neil Pointon, who came into the side when JJ was struggling to stabilise a leaky defence. Neil had been at several clubs in England, most notably Everton and Manchester City, and had a wonderful left foot – many Jambos will recall his fine goal against Rangers at Tynecastle.

Two incidents involving him stick out in my mind. The first was at Hampden, before reconstruction, in a cup semi-final against Aberdeen in 1996. It was a dour match, typical of many others I have witnessed at the National Stadium, but Neil was at the centre of one of the game's big talking points. In the second half, with Hearts leading, Joe Miller took off down the left side when he was met by Neil. I have seen many tackles, but this one just looked like a random kick and the winger

Stevie Fulton, Steven Boyack, Steven Pressley, Scott Severin, Robbie Neilson and Austin McCann, pre-season 2001–02.

was carried off with what turned out to be a minor fracture. I thought, 'He's off,' but the officials saw things differently and he remained on, with only a booking.

Hearts have always been involved in controversy: protests, takeovers, fines, suspensions, boardroom spats, visits from sheriff's officers are all run of the mill affairs in Gorgie – but four players sent off at Ibrox? Did this fit the mould? A phlegmatic David Weir and the stripling Ritchie were hardly candidates for an early bath. Pasquale had a lot of 'previous' and would always be the bookies' favourite to be sent packing. To be dismissed for assaulting a goal post was something new, yet this was Pointon's heinous crime. The linesman, as they were then called, was culpable in that he drew referee Evans' attention to the incident. By then, I think Mr Evans just wanted to go home for a cuddle. Thankfully further damage failed to be inflicted on the battling, shell-shocked visitors with the score remaining 2-0.

With Gary Naysmith leaving for Everton in 2000, Craig Levein had an enormous hole on the left side of his defence to fill. As stated previously, this manager was never shy when it came to taking a risk on a player, and enticing Stéphane Mahé to Gorgie was certainly something of a gamble. The former Celtic favourite arrived with a reputation for being passionate and honest. Training days were never going to be the same for the next couple of seasons, with staff and players alike soon learning more about French expletives than they ever did from Messrs Rousset, Adam and Guérin. French players of this era had done National Service in the military and, combined with the discipline of professional sport, this character building gave them an advantage over British lads who were more likely to be cosseted from an early age.

The great pity about Stéphane's signing was that it came too late for him to establish himself as a Hearts hero, but the 50 or so games in which he performed were to give the supporters a taste of what he had been like in his prime.

Athletes' tendons tend to show their age more than other anatomical areas and Stéphane's body struggled to cope with the advancing years. Irrespective of what treatment was tried, he could not shake off a problem in the lower leg which tends to affect a large number of 'elderly' players. To make matters worse, a business venture he had become involved with was going belly-up, which saw mental issues exacerbate his situation. Physical problems linked to those of a mental nature make rehabilitation doubly difficult and alas, a fair measure of 'dodgy' financial advice created a mess which brought an end to a fine career.

Often on Saturday mornings before home games I would review youngsters who had signed 'S' forms for the Hearts. Boys who are aged between 12 and 16 play an enormous amount of games and participate in training sessions two to three times a week, so it's no surprise they incur a variety of problems associated with growth cycles and overuse. There is no point bemoaning the demise of street football, when kids would go in for their tea and return rested and refreshed, or when their maws would throw them a jeely piece from a tenement window. Today's necessity is to educate coaches a little more in children's physiology and to place less emphasis on winning Mickey Mouse tournaments. I have seen scores of youth players with irritated bone growth plates through overuse of the attached muscles. The lad who presented himself on this particular Saturday walked like a sailor and had the cut of a stormtrooper. When he walked and ran, his feet were using half the sole and half the outside upper of his boots. This was Scott Severin, who was to become one of Hearts' finest home-bred midfielders in recent times. Youngsters who are promoted to the first team and play regularly pick up injuries more often than their senior colleagues. Natural strength, dedication and a do-or-die attitude ensured Seve would have a successful career in football, although I was saddened to learn of his serious leg break while playing for Dundee United early in season 2011–12.

Selected for the first team in a match at Fir Park, he was soon in the thick of the action. The home team would be well apprised about the young rookie in midfield, the usual advice going something like: 'Let him know he's in a game'; 'Rattle him a couple of times to welcome him to the Premier League'; and 'You're never good enough to play for the Hearts'. One of the old chestnuts coming from a seasoned performer to a debutant was: 'Ye'll need a ticket tae get intae this gemme, son!' Any fears about this lad's ability to handle the big time were dispelled when he attacked a high ball into the box, after which the opposition centre half left the field nursing a broken jaw. By the way, a commitment to winning the ball can, in itself, protect players from injury.

A month or so before the start of the 2002 World Cup, a request from Moray House and the Department of Physical Education arrived at Tynecastle. In conjunction with a film company, a sports scientist wanted to conduct a series of neurophysiological tests involving a pro soccer player who, when wired to a computer, would visualise shots at goal just prior to kicking the ball. I was all for this experiment. The club would be seen to be forward thinking by supplying the player and I might learn something to my advantage. The obvious player, to my mind, would be Seve, in that he was every inch a professional.

The day came round for the experiment. On our arrival we were greeted by the Moray House staff and then we got down to a warm-up routine. This completed, the scientist proceeded to attach a number of wires to Seve's head, which were then connected to a computer. After a few minutes of fine tuning, a football was produced. The idea was that

Seve would be told where to aim for on a set of goals. The 'postage stamp', or top right or left corner, was selected. I could see that the film crew were not expecting any consistency from the player, but the next few minutes enlightened them. Getting the nod from the scientist, Seve tried one. It missed the goals. I could sense a few smirks behind our backs. After that opener, Seve's hard-wiring kicked in. For the next ten minutes every shot was visualised and smacked into one angle of bar and post or the other. How did they like *these* apples? The session ended with a round of applause.

Afterwards I received assurances from both crew and boffin that we would be informed as to when this would be shown on national TV and that I would be sent a copy of the test results. We paid our own taxi back to Tynecastle. Yes, I'm still waiting for the results, and as for the TV coverage – a three-second clip was included in the introduction at the start of the programme.

Robert Louis Stevenson is often credited as having introduced the split personality into literature in *The Strange Case of Dr Jekyll and Mr Hyde* (1886). Or did James Hogg beat him to it with his *Private Memoirs and Confessions of a Justified Sinner*, which appeared in 1824? Either way, I would suggest that this duality is not confined to the Scottish character. In football, I have often observed how dramatically many players' personalities are transformed when they cross that white line. Thereafter, for 90 minutes, a drug takes over their normal psyche – adrenaline. The chemistry of this basic lifesaver is beyond my scope but I would suggest that without its presence in the body, football would not be the game it is.

Joe Jordan brought Ian Baird to Tynecastle to complement John Robertson's striking capabilities. He joined up with the club at Dingwall, where Hearts were preparing for their first full season under the Jordan–Connor management team. When I first met Ian I found him to be reserved, polite and articulate, but that was one side of him, and I was soon to see the other. As a youngster at Southampton, he had looked after former European Footballer of the Year Kevin Keegan's boots, but it was difficult to see whether KK's habit of total professionalism might have rubbed off on him. The season got under way with Ian in the thick of things.

Tynecastle may not have been what he had been used to at his former clubs, Leeds and Middlesbrough, but he certainly acquainted himself with the spartan gymnasium and the speed ball, which he took to like a duck to water. On the park he was a huge presence, making it difficult for goalkeepers and centre backs to keep their eye on the ball with him on the rampage. From time to time when watching him perform I was reminded of sports reporter and columnist Ian Wood's description of the Hearts team in *The Scotsman*: after a game at Dens Park a few years earlier he wrote that the team, before battering the door down, first should try the handle.

Shortly after his signing, Ian sustained a nasty ankle twist at Parkhead. He played on, but by the time he came off at the end it was grossly swollen. Continental players would have been out until Christmas and beyond with something like this. Not Ian. 'Al, get your fingers into it and shift that swelling! Just strap it up, give me some Brufen and I'll play.' And he did. As he got fitter and became accustomed to the Scottish game, he relished the service from the likes of Eamonn and JC. To give an example of his menace, during a derby encounter JR crossed a ball from the left when attacking the away end (Gorgie Road at that time). The ball should have been a 'John Brough', a one-handed fielding job for Budgie Burridge, but Ian loomed up in his peripheral vision, with the result that the ball bounced into the net without further contact.

Ian had a facial expression when penalised, rightly or wrongly, of persecution: 'Who – me?' Perhaps as a young professional he had been battered by older, wiser defenders, hence the look of enduring injustice. Two anecdotes involving the striker linger in my memory. In a warm-up prior to a cup quarter-final against Falkirk at Tynecastle he injured his thigh. As the team lines had been submitted it would be up to the opposition management to give permission for another substitute to be named. This was none other than Jim Jefferies, who was alleged to have said: 'No problem – but it can't be Scott Crabbe!'

In the other incident Hearts were playing Aberdeen at Pittodrie.

Nicky Walker had the gloves and at that time a second keeper could not be stripped for the bench. Once again there was an injury during the warm-up. This time it was the 'roly-poly'. Nicky had torn a calf muscle. A volunteer was required to fill the role of the incapacitated Walker and Ian was the only player willing to take on the No. 1 jersey. With his defence protecting him well, he didn't have a lot to do in the game and couldn't be faulted for the goals lost. Hearts did lose but the authorities were jolted into action, recognising that such predicaments had an effect on the entertainment value of the game. Still, a year was to pass before substitute goalkeepers were allowed on the bench without a reduction in the number of substitute outfield players.

Part of the shake-up following Joe Jordan's departure as manager was Ian moving on, this time to Bristol City. Scottish keepers and centre halves would be glad to see the back of this particular Mr Hyde.

In the war horse category I have to mention a fine lad called Róbert Tomaschek, signed by Jim Jefferies from Bratislava. This player was a snip. Tall, slim and athletic, he had captained the Slovakian national team as well as Slovan Bratislava. This sort of recognition was a sound endorsement of his character and it was just a pity he had not arrived a couple of years earlier. He soon established himself in the team and life in Scotland appeared to suit his wife and family. A change of management did not have any influence on his attitude and a mutual liking grew between him and Mr Levein. Personally, I thought he was a 'diamond'.

At Parkhead one afternoon Róbert was chasing a long, high ball into his own half of the field. Lesser players might have headed or 'emptied' it into the crowd. Róbert chose to control the ball on his instep in mid air. Disaster! As he landed his knee over-extended. The mechanism of injury to a physiotherapist is crucial to understanding what might be wrong and there was no doubt in my mind this was the end of the season for Róbert.

Magnetic resonance imaging takes the guesswork out of articular conditions. The scan made it obvious that reconstructive surgery was urgently required. But where would this be performed? I was, invariably, of the view that the club should 'shop local'; after all, Edinburgh was at the forefront of medicine. The logistics also made sense – complications could be dealt with easily and follow-up appointments would be routine.

The adage 'he who pays the piper calls the tune' comes to mind. The board chose to send Róbert to that centre of soccer activity – *Colorado*! He was packed off on a long flight, probably the longest in his life, to have his reconstructive surgery. What he thought of this was kept close to his chest; if the cost meant anything, he was getting treatment out of the top drawer.

On his return, with enough paper work to choke a horse, Dr Melvin and I got down to planning his route to full recovery. Rehabilitation can be soul destroying for the patient and this is where the staff involved earn their corn, by addressing the mind as well as the body.

I made sure that I visited Robert's house to meet his wife and his two young children in order to reassure her that everything possible was being done for her man. As Christmas 2002 approached Róbert had progressed through the programme to the stage where he could jog. Lay people and football coaches often attach great significance to being able to run during rehab. Wrong – no healthy person forgets how to run. Psychologically this weight bearing activity may have some value, but ensuring that the limb involved is ready to take at least three to five times the body weight with every alternate stride (when walking) is of critical importance.

Coming from a former Eastern Bloc country where the Socialists had been obsessed with success in all sports, Robert, I thought, might benefit from some diversional therapy, ie something which, to the patient, might seem unrelated to his injury. When I asked if he had ever played table tennis, Róbert answered, 'A little,' which was rather like Viv Richards saying he could hit a cricket ball.

On Christmas Eve, when most folks were hurrying to make last-minute purchases before enjoying some family down-time, I was on my way to buy a 'full Monty' table-tennis table. Purchase made, this huge package was humphed into the club van. My intention was to install it on the concourse behind the old grandstand. Just unwrap it, unfold the legs, and before you could say 'ping-pong' we would be in action – or so I imagined.

This table was a piece of work; there must have been 50 parts to it, not including the nuts and bolts. Former engineer John Murray (now director of the Hearts Youth Academy) and former plumber John McGlynn, the reserve and youth coach, were summoned to help a hapless physio assemble Robert's Christmas present.

When the players returned from their seasonal break it was the ground staff who were first to take on the Slovakian *wunderkind* at table tennis. He whipped them all! It wasn't long before the management got a whiff of what was going on and they duly appeared to take control of the situation – nobody but Levein and Houston was going to get near that table! Well, Róbert did get a game in the doubles. In a lighter moment we did think of running a scam where an acknowledged player would be invited to take on our novice Slovak, just like Fast Eddie did in *The Hustler*, but it remained a thought.

A reserve match at Dens Park marked Robert's return. He performed well, considering how long he had been out of competitive football, and marked the occasion by scoring a goal. His attitude had been wonderful throughout his rehab but I could tell he was unhappy with his recovery. Eventually he visited a master-surgeon in Edinburgh who trimmed the Colorado graft which, it was felt, was more of a skier's graft than one intended for a multi-directional footballer. By the season's end Róbert had had enough, deciding at the age of 30 it was time to hang up his boots. Injuries, apart from being painful and disabling, disrupt family life and for most of us our family is life's priority.

Outside of playing professional football, his knee would be adequate. In Slovakia he was still a top personality and perhaps offers had arrived for him which were too inviting to refuse. When he announced he was quitting I was saddened by his decision, but I suppose he'd had a guid kick at the baw.

When a new manager takes over a team, one of the first things he does is formulate a plan for bringing in his own players. As Tony Mowbray's ill-fated reign at Celtic showed, such moves can be chastening experiences. At the end of the Jefferies era in 2000, Craig Levein had set about breathing new life into the Tynecastle squad. Tried and tested players are expensive but sometimes a gem can be uncovered who, with a little attention and proper man-management, becomes a valuable asset.

During his playing days, Levein had made a huge leap from Cowdenbeath to reach the pinnacle of his career by playing for Scotland, and he was heading to repeat the process as a manager. He quickly demonstrated he was a gaffer willing to take risks with his squad additions. Prime examples were Paul Hartley, a man of many clubs, not least city rivals Hibs, and Republic of Ireland internationalist Alan Maybury, who had sustained injuries to both legs which saw him plummet from playing in the Champions League to struggling along in Leeds United's third team.

Then there was Phil Stamp. When it became apparent his godfather was Roy 'Chubby' Brown, we should have known it wasn't going to be plain sailing with this chap around. His solid physique drew comparisons with former Hearts and Celtic star Mike Galloway. If anything, Phil had more flexibility, but Mike was more versatile and could perform at centre half just as easily as at centre forward. They both had a seriously daft streak. Phil arrived just when the Hearts Football Academy was opening at Riccarton on the outskirts of Edinburgh. The Scottish Premier League meant something of an adjustment for the powerful midfielder who had played in the 1997 FA Cup Final. He gave us a glimpse of the pampered life of the top flight professionals down south when he told us how the Middlesbrough squad headed to the Cheltenham National Hunt Festival – by helicopter hired by manager Bryan Robson and captain Paul Ince, the former Manchester United star.

Phil had indeed rubbed shoulders with some big hitters and was not short of a tale or two. As a teenager up against Sheffield Wednesday at Hillsborough, at a corner kick for Middlesbrough, he stood on Carlton Palmer's toes – perhaps not the shrewdest move he ever made. The response was interesting and a little lateral. As his ear was pulled in the direction of Palmer's mouth, the big guy hissed: 'You little ginger foock! Coom out wi' me after game and ah'll show you foockin' round all my foockin' houses!'

Later during his stay at Hearts, the club supplied new accommodation for Stamp. All was well until he decided to try home cooking. To augment his kitchen tools, he splashed out on a barbecue. This particular piece of apparatus had wheels, one would imagine to allow it to be pushed from the shed to the garden and then back again after the social gathering. Not so with this one – it was pushed into the lounge, where it was lit and used! I recollect the emergency services being involved and the letting agency being 'flaming' mad.

The stocky Englishman brought his dog with him when he moved to Edinburgh and he exercised this little fellow regularly – and at odd hours. One very early morning at Cramond, this man's best friend took to the high seas when the tide was ebbing. This meant that it was going to take more of a Michael Phelps effort than a doggy paddle to get the pooch back to the beach. Brave as a lion but daft as a brush, Phil took the plunge. It's still not clear who saved who, but both got back to terra firma. Soaked through, he staggered back to the main road to hail a taxi. One eventually stopped, offering salvation until the cabbie recognised who he was: 'You're Phil Stamp, you scored against the Hibs... you can fucking walk!'

Phil's cross-field passes, played with nonchalance and power, were something to behold as they were usually struck with the outside of his foot. The famous interplay in November 2002 between him and Neil Janczyk at Easter Road attacking the away end comes to mind, with Phil completing the exchange by stroking the ball home for a late winner. He didn't surprise anyone on the bench by getting sent off for his celebrations, although most would agree he was harshly treated by referee Willie Young. Football is an emotional sport and if you can't celebrate with your own fans after scoring a last-minute winner against your fiercest rivals, why bother pulling on your boots in the first place?

CHAPTER 14
Pair of Aces

CRAIG BROWN ONCE said that the most perfect pass he'd ever seen was played at Ibrox by Stevie Fulton during his spell at Falkirk. The love affair between Stevie and the managerial duo of Jefferies and Brown continued after they left The Bairns to go to Tynecastle. A natural left-footed player is always an asset to a side, in that he can balance the team, but this was not the main reason for this shrewd signing.

Fulton was a wonderful passer of the ball with a fabulous burst of speed. It's possible that, had he been handled more sympathetically at Celtic, his first club, he might have been at Parkhead for life. He had an ongoing battle to control his weight and it could be that Celtic felt that this would limit his future contribution. Yet Liam Brady, the former Arsenal star and an ex-manager of The Hoops, who knows a thing or two about the game, reputedly observed: 'Fulton was as good as Paul McStay and John Collins put together.' Quite an assertion. When Fulton was shown the door out of Celtic Park and pointed in the direction of Bolton Wanderers he must have been broken-hearted. It didn't happen for him there in Lancashire; nobody loved him – he was a sonsie boy. To add further insult to injury he was put out on loan to Peterborough. It couldn't have got much worse but at least with The Posh he was still playing football.

Jim Jefferies plucked him from this situation to give his side at Brockville a bit of class. By the time he arrived at Tynecastle in autumn 1995, Fulton had spent a year playing with honest professionals. At 25 years of age, it was time to show his maturity at a higher level but the Jambos were having another difficult season.

Somewhere along the road Stevie had picked up the sobriquet

'Baggio'. Some people were quick to say how difficult it must have been to be paired with a superstar, which the Italian indeed was: 'Il Divino Codino' played for the top three Italian teams, AC and Inter Milan and Juventus. Most Jambos growing up at Tynecastle in the 1980s must have heard the cry 'Ziccoooh' roaring out of the old shed when Walter Kidd set off on a foray up the line. Being compared to the famous Brazilian didn't do Walter any harm, as he went on to play over 400 games at Hearts. The name 'Baggio' stuck to Stevie, albeit in the abbreviated form, 'Badge!' I preferred this to 'Fulters' which, for my money, has a public school ring to it like 'Jonners' or 'Aggers' (the late Brian Johnston and Jonathan Agnew, *if* you follow cricket).

The quality at Hearts was still high: the rump of the '86 squad remained in Mackay, Robertson and Colquhoun, who were strengthened in defence by the class of David McPherson who had re-signed the previous season, again from Rangers. As we know, the management were denied the services of Craig Levein through injury early in the season against Dunfermline, and the spectre of the previous season's dalliance with relegation hovered over the club.

Good players are accepted readily by other good players; winning becomes more frequent and bonuses accumulate. Stevie's qualities were touch, vision, strength and an explosive burst of speed which 'killed' opponents. His team-mates knew when they gave him the ball it would stick and the resulting pass would go to a player in maroon.

As a well-known player at Old Trafford is finding out, when the 25-year marker looms, everything gets that little bit harder. More rest is required, food has to be selected carefully and family life can, at times, weigh heavily. Stevie was a solid lad, his build came with birth. I was often asked to monitor his weight and discover what he was stoking himself with. It was a slog. Eventually I came to the conclusion that a happy Baggio played better than a leaner, unhappy one.

After a poor performance at St Johnstone's McDiarmid Park one night, there was a serious post-mortem in the away dressing room. It was a long, drawn out tongue-lashing for all involved. Whoever designed this newish stadium must have been told not to allow the visitors too much space or comfort, perhaps working on the psychological aspects

Gary Mackay gives a celebratory piggy-back to Kenny Black.
© Eric McCowat Sports Photo Archive.

of overcrowding. The players were getting cold but nobody moved during the tirade. Nobody, that is, except Stevie, who stood up and stripped off, at the same time putting in his tuppence worth about the game. With a flourish he threw his knickers into a gaping hamper and stood like a male stripper in his blushing pink birthday suit for a very pregnant moment, then turned on his heel and made the short journey to the showers.

Oh dear, here was a chosen son throwing the toys out of the pram, spitting out the dummy, dissenting in the face of the manager.

The response was immediate: 'Stevie, if you don't get your fucking erse back in here it'll cost you a fucking week's wages!'

From the showers, now running, came the riposte: 'You can stick yer wages!'

Advantage Fulton. Mr Jefferies to serve.

'Stevie, now it's a month's wages.' Deuce.

'And how long is it tae Christmas?' Baggio emerged, resumed his seat, dripping. Game, set and match to Jefferies in the face of an uncharacteristic outburst – Badge was a humorous guy and not easily roused.

After a season with the Jambos, Stevie would return to his *alma mater* in a league cup final at Celtic Park (when Hampden was undergoing reconstruction). Here was a chance for Stevie to prevent Rangers from winning a major trophy on the hallowed turf of his first club. The game started poorly for the Jambos, with Rangers going two goals ahead very early, perhaps not surprisingly given that the weather and road conditions had combined to delay the Hearts bus. A hurried preparation followed, bearing out my view that the venue for a major final always favours a Glasgow-based team. As half time approached, Hearts were edging into things, with Stevie striking a low left footer across Andy Goram. 2-1. Game on.

The result of the match hinged on two incidents, a critical stop by Goram denying Hearts' Colin Cameron an equaliser and a throw-in awarded to the wrong side which gave the erratic genius Paul Gascoigne the opportunity to increase Rangers' lead. It had been a close match, ending 4-3 to the Teddys, but no cigars for the Gorgie team. Hearts and Stevie would have to wait for almost another two years for their day in the sun.

A little less than a year later a player who had graced the Tynecastle turf for 16 seasons left Hearts. It was a sad day for Gary Mackay, his contribution to the club having far outweighed what he received in return. The records show how many times (640) he played for the Jambos. The anguish of 1986 and the clutch of semi-finals and finals he played in without a win must have been crushing. He left the club with nothing but a pair of boots under his arm.

One of my favourite anecdotes about this fine player relates to a pre-season trip to Dublin which took place after Mackay left Hearts. For me, Ireland was always preferable to some of the humourless places I visited on the Continent with Hearts. Our Irish cousins speak roughly the same language, cook the same grub and have similar plumbing arrangements. The style of football closely resembles the Scottish product and the pitches are well watered. Ideal. And of course, there is a brand of fun which is sometimes lacking over here. On arriving at Dalymount Park to play the Bohemians, I asked what time the kick-off was. The reply: 'Oh, about three, maybe. Will that do you all right?'

There is another side to the city, as you would expect. The team bus was waiting to make a right turn into the hotel across a busy dual carriageway in Naas when I noticed a wooden cross stuck in the middle of the central reservation. I mentioned this to the driver, asking if there had been a recent fatality. His reply was chilling. 'That's where Veronica Guerin was assassinated last year. A guy on the pillion of a motorbike shot her six times with a .357 Magnum.' Guerin was an investigative journalist who had threatened to expose members of the criminal gangs in Dublin.

One Sunday morning Hearts first team coach Paul Hegarty (who formerly had a distinguished career with Dundee United) and I took the players who would not be performing in the afternoon to a public park to give them a 'blow'. During a lull in the session we watched a man exercise his dog by hitting a ball with a hurling stick for the animal to retrieve. Could he hit that ball! I enquired if he had done this before and a bit of craic developed: 'Oh, so it's from Edinburgh you're from. Is it the Hearts then?' When we answered in the affirmative, he asked if Gary Mackay was in the party. Gary was a household name here after his famous strike for Scotland against the Bulgarians which secured a place for Jack Charlton's Republic of Ireland team in the European Championships in 1988.

There were, I'm sure, many reasons for Gary's playing success, not least his technical ability and vision in the game. Straight from former Hearts wing half Scott Leitch's coaching tutorial: 'A good player with the ball will see three passes and instinctively play the right one.' This is an apt description of Gary Mackay.

Alex MacDonald's influence loomed large. He instilled in Gary's young mind the need for hard work, absolute physical fitness and a good attitude. Along the way to this condition he was inspired by the great sprinter George McNeil and his coaching companion Bert Logan.

To become a 'box to box' player like MacDonald, a great deal of work had to be done in the close season when most players of that era were taking it easy. Gary punished himself at Meadowbank Stadium summer after summer and the results were there for all to see. In preseason training he was 'flying' – he was a manager's delight.

Some of the more subtle aspects of his fitness needed to be addressed prophylactically, particularly the health of the lower back, which is like the New Street Station of the body in that all the upward and downward stresses pass through these five crucial lumbar vertebrae.

Short hamstrings often increase the wear and tear in the lumbar area and by lengthening this group of muscles, the stress can be reduced.(The three hamstring muscles extend from the 'sit-upon' bone on the pelvis, down the back of the thigh to gain attachments behind the knee.) Gary took on a stretch programme to remedy this 'shortcoming'. Within a few weeks the positive results were obvious, even to the player. The lesson Gary would pass on to younger players is to be receptive to advice from all sources when offered.

In a game which is becoming more athletic by the year, mobility and stamina are common denominators. Talent gets players spotted and 'in the door', but that is only the beginning. Without his application Gary would have drifted down the leagues, as so many boys do. I've seen lads who can play keepy-up in a broom cupboard but lack the mindset to progress to a highly rewarded occupation. An away game at Fir Park saw Gary dropped completely from the team, not even on the bench, and this was more than the Hearts-daft youngster could take. Roddy McDonald pulled a hamstring in the warm-up. A search for Gary came up with zip; even the canteen at Motherwell, renowned for its 'fly cemeteries' and apple tarts, yielded nothing. Somehow he had bummed a lift back to Edinburgh. The manager did not mete out a harsh punishment, realising how crushed he had felt.

The build-up to any derby match sometimes outweighs the occasion. This match against the Hibs was being covered extensively by press, radio and TV. On the day the sun shone. Tynecastle was packed, with famous former players from both sides in attendance. Fifteen minutes into the action it was obvious that Gary was not himself. Pre-match nerves had taken control and caused him to overheat. He was burnt out before he got onto the park. Learning how to control the adrenaline was another aspect of his game which he discovered the hard way. On that occassion, he was taken off after 20 minutes.

Gary stayed clear of major injury problems because of his attention to rest, nutrition and personal fitness; he also possessed a great pair of legs, with tight knee joints and superb protective quadriceps. Honest knocks come every player's way. Contusions from heads, knees, elbows and studs are commonplace and prominent bony areas like eyebrows, the upper nose and cheek bones are regularly traumatised. Gary had both cheek bones broken by Hibernian defender Gordon Hunter and Celtic's Billy Stark.

He was not the type who shirked a challenge although, to be fair, he was not a defender in the true sense. For example, how often did this forward-thinking player surge from defence to take a long throw from Henry Smith in his stride to set up an instant counter attack?

I would wager that it will be a long time until we see a contribution like Gary's being made to a single team. He belonged to a nucleus of Hearts players who shared a cameraderie on and off the pitch. Without that fellowship at the core, success is hard to come by for any football club.

CHAPTER 15
A Trophy at Last

CUP WINNING IN SCOTLAND, particularly the Scottish Cup, is made extremely difficult due to the presence of Glasgow Rangers and Glasgow Celtic: playing either of these monsters at Ibrox or Celtic Park in a knockout competition means that an exit visa is invariably included in the away ticket allocation. Playing them at home is the lesser team's chance, as was proved in Rangers' case by two defeats at Berwick and Hamilton.

At Tynecastle, the Jambos had at least four wins in cup games in the '80s and '90s, two against Celtic and two against Rangers. At some point during a cup campaign teams have to beat either or both of the Old Firm. At home a real chance exists, whereas in a semi-final or final on a neutral ground (if you can describe Hampden as such) the odds lengthen. Why? Well, the big teams are there regularly (I may be mistaken but I don't recall either of the Old Firm playing a semi on a ground outside Glasgow). I have witnessed three or four semi-finals at Tynecastle involving both Dundee clubs, Aberdeen, Hibernian and St Johnstone – a truly neutral venue for all these sides.

As I have mentioned, Hampden was undergoing reconstruction in 1998 and Celtic Park became the venue for the Scottish Cup Final. I felt that this would suit Hearts better as we had had some, though not many, victories on this pitch. With the hosts less than pleased at the prospect of their bitter rivals lifting a national trophy on their grass, neutrality was being tinged with 'home advantage' for Hearts.

Before we could dream of any glorious afternoon in the east end of Glasgow, there was the small matter of a semi-final against First Division underdogs Falkirk. Semi-finals are nervy affairs for the favourites and after scoring early Hearts were given a bit of a going over before eventually conceding an equaliser to Kevin McAllister's fine strike. A replay seemed to be on the cards but the speed of Neil McCann caught The Bairns on the front foot and Stéphane Adam bundled his cross home via a shin. Neil himself finished the tie, running on to a through ball and outpacing former Hearts player Neil Berry, who I thought might have pulled down the flying winger. He didn't, which was a great sporting gesture, and McCann, one on one with the keeper, made the finish look easy.

So it was to be another final against a strong Rangers team but Hearts, at last, had the best blend of youth and experience since the team of the mid-'80s.

This squad assembled by Jefferies and Brown had a perfect balance. Gary Naysmith, Paul Ritchie, Steve Fulton and Neil McCann were all naturally left-sided. Thomas Flögel, Colin Cameron and Stefano Salvatori still had their midfield legs. David Weir and David McPherson were tall and would be the match for crosses and high balls, while Adam and Gilles Rousset made up the set. In John Robertson's words, Stéphane knew the game inside out, being not only aware of the runs to make but also when to make them. His game was unselfish. He made space for his team-mates, allowing them to make easy passes. Gilles was in his 30s, with the experience to make the right decisions in fractions of a second. Another incentive for 'le grand gardien' was the chance to end his career with a winner's medal, having failed to win anything during his time in France.

JJ's preparations for the Celtic Park showdown included a journey to a billet in William Shakespeare's neck of the woods. In the unlikely setting of the National Farmers' Union Mutual Headquarters' Sports Centre, the squad trained twice a day on good grass and magnificent buffet lunches were served in a huge staff canteen a furlong from the training field. Despite being close to the National Theatre in Stratford, watching *Hamlet* was the last thing on our minds, while the other great Dane, Laudrup, who had tortured us two years earlier in the '96 Scottish Cup Final, was never going to be far from our thoughts or dreams. His pace, control and unique balance coupled with a low

The Scottish Cup winner Adam with the trophy and his medal in his right hand.
© Eric McCowat Sports Photo Archive.

centre of gravity was, for the Ibrox faithful, a joy to behold. Still, if he didn't get the ball...

This hideout must have deterred the Scottish press bloodhounds, as I don't recall a visit from anyone representing a newspaper apart from Martin Dempster from the local Edinburgh rag. Not that we were totally neglected; the BBC presenter Hazel Irvine appeared one evening, which was a real pleasure – she even gave an impromptu piano recital. Hazel has a Vera Lynn quality, in that everyone she speaks to feels as

Twenty-four hours after Hearts' Scottish Cup triumph, fans gathered outside St Giles'
Cathedral to see the team on their victory tour of Edinburgh.

though he or she is the absolute focus of her attention. You might say,
'But that's her job.' Well, I would say there are many in the media who
could use some of her innate ability.

With 72 hours left until the final, our main worry was Colin
Cameron. Any Jambo will tell you that this ruthless little Fifer had
transformed Hearts' midfield with his lung-bursting runs into the
box. Off the pitch he was just as crusty and would let you know in no
uncertain terms when his tea was served unstirred.

Playing with that all-action style puts a huge strain on the union between the trunk and lower limbs and Colin was feeling the effects of a long season. Running is all very well – in a straight line – but when turning, jumping, jostling and kicking, with all the subtleties involved, it's not surprising if 'the wheel comes off the barra'. Colin needed rest and the summer would bring with it a chance to heal the aching lower abdominal muscles. Apart from this problem, he was raring to go. He had been denied another League Cup winner's medal (he was a winner with Raith Rovers when they beat Celtic in the League Cup Final in 1994) by Andy Goram's heel. Now there was a chance of winning the 'big cup' *and* he was more than aware of the accompanying bonus having been at the final with Raith which led to the mighty Bayern Munich playing at Stark's Park in the UEFA Cup.

Hearts had used Dalmahoy Country Club as a place to stay pre-match for the 1996 final, but after that hammering there was no chance of this golfers' hangout being used again, at least in this century, so the night before the big day we were taken to Dunblane.

A bright sunny Saturday morning arrived with its 'butterflies'. Everyone was resplendent in new suits and shoes – I don't recall if there were lucky white heather button-holes; in the past they had been the harbingers of defeat.

At Celtic Park the normal match routine kicked in. After so many years the preparations are hard-wired into the brain and neuromuscular system. Strappings, rubs and stretches were all gone through, sometimes as a necessary, tangible support, but more often as a ritual like the final 'Ave Maria', or lovers' kiss, or checking that 'your powder's dry' for the umpteenth time. Vick's VapoRub on the shirt front and under the chin, Vaseline above the eyebrows, all rings wrapped with zinc oxide tape, tighten the boot studs, urinate and defecate – adrenaline gets rid of the excess baggage (in the words of my grandfather, 'better an empty hoose than a bad tenant'). It was all part of the normal build-up. Enter referee Willie Young, a solicitor by profession and contrary by nature. Check the boots and by now 'the hounds were baying', all that energy brought to the boil and ready to be released. *Showtime!*

It was a perfect climax to the season. There was a huge crowd and the sun shining as it did made a wonderful case for summer football. A touch of Hollywood was added by the attendance of Robert Duvall, who must have been impressed with Stevie Fulton's peroxide hair job, which was a ringer for Roy Batty's, the leader of the Nexus-6 replicant group in *Blade Runner*.

I am not going to attempt to describe the match besides mentioning Cameron's penalty, which was well clear of Goram's heel, and Stéphane's strike into the ground, which didn't look spectacular until you see it again – and again and again, as many Hearts fans did later that night. There was a sadness to the occasion though, as John Robertson, named as a substitute, was the only survivor from 1986 who did not get to perform.

Towards the end, the mobility and defensive heading abilities of Jim Hamilton were more appropriate due to the pressure of Rangers' late surge in an attempt to save the match. Gary Naysmith went down with a head knock and somewhat reluctantly I went on. 'If you're no paralysed, get up – we could lose this in injury time!' I said.

My experience told me that his nervous system was intact. Characteristically, Willie Young allowed play to continue for what seemed the rest of the afternoon but in fact was only five minutes. (I refused to look at my watch, which I had brought in the hope that it would be a talisman for the Hearts: it was my father's, a gift from my mother on their wedding day 59 years earlier.) When Willie finally blew the whistle for full-time, all I wanted was to share that moment with my family, who were in the stand, and who had supported me through all the disappointments of the previous 16 years.

Adam was nowhere to be seen. He had been substituted but even a hardened pro like him couldn't bear to sit with us to endure the stress of the final minutes and he had raced off to the dressing room. My memory of his reappearance is of a totally wiped-out Frenchman standing outside the tunnel with his mouth wide open in disbelief. The franc finally dropped as he took off onto the pitch to join his teammates in an explosion of joy and relief.

In the dressing room after the cup presentation, there was more than the usual mayhem. The 'double yolkers' – the directors – got in on the celebrations with their state-of-the-art cameras, which they were entitled to do as they had been through the pain of the previous losing finals.

When the stour settled and players were being randomly selected for drug testing, a chill ran down my spine. What if one of the squad had taken a 'wee hurry up'? Oh boy, could victory be snatched from Hearts after so many failures? I needn't have worried though – the total professional, Gilles Rousset, was asked to provide a specimen; Stevie 'Baggio' Fulton was the other player selected and I was confident this fine wing half would be drug-free.

There was going to be a long wait for the guys to produce their samples and so after tidying my kit I went for a wander and noticed a TV in the foyer showing the match highlights. Professor Hillis, the Rangers medical official, was seated nearby. As often happens with match reports on radio or TV, you never hear the score or a mention of the incident which is of interest to you, so I turned to the professor and asked him if it had been a penalty. He replied: 'The referee said it was!' indicating to me that as far as the opposing bench were concerned, the foul by Weir on McCoist was not regarded as having been committed in the box and apparently accepting that Ferguson's illegal tackle on Fulton was, leading to Cameron's expertly taken spot kick.

Another Rangers official I met was Campbell Ogilvie and he was sincere in his congratulations when I remarked what a huge occasion this was for Heart of Midlothian. To balance my comment I was put in mind of a remark made by Graeme Souness as top man at Anfield when Liverpool were playing Aberdeen at Pittodrie. An official of the home team had commented to him what a big game it was. 'Yes, it is,' came the reply, 'for Aberdeen!'

Eventually Stevie and Gilles produced the goods, so to speak, enabling us to return to Gorgie where the faithful were installed, eagerly awaiting an event they could tell their grandchildren about. After a wonderful evening I walked home with my daughters. Halfway along Dalry Road we spotted goal hero Adam and his wee French *copain* strolling along, unassuming and unrecognised, as if it had just been a good day at the office.

The oldest football trophy in the world, the cup was something of a Holy Grail, so everybody and their dog wanted a shot of it and I was no exception. But before I could get my hands on it, someone else had taken it on a tour of East Lothian where, it was rumoured, it had spent the night in a coal bunker.

From the management team of 1956 there was only one survivor, Donald McLeod, who had been assistant to John Harvey Snr. He was being looked after in a nursing home in Penicuik and as a gesture as much to his family as to him, John Harvey Jnr and I did a heist by taking the trophy to the home where Donald, his family and the staff could have a little celebration of their own.

On its way back to Tynecastle, the cup stopped off at chez Rae, where more photos were taken during the kids' school lunch break! As Paul Hegarty once said to me: 'There are so many disappointments in the game. When something good happens, enjoy it to the full.' He was right, on both counts.

CHAPTER 16
Dutch Master

SHORT OF FIRE-POWER, the Hearts were on the hunt for a new striker. The years of hard graft and selfless running had caught up with Stéphane Adam who, in a total of 145 appearances, had scored 33 goals for the club. When he left the Jam Tarts his weight-bearing joints were in good order but it had become clear that the longer he continued to play the more likely he was to succumb to muscular problems. Therapists of all shapes and sizes, including myself, were consulted, but advancing years brought down this cup hero.

Ever since JR had left in 1998, finding a replacement who could also deliver 20 goals a season had been the quest for Hearts' talent scouts. Millions of pounds are exchanged by clubs desperate for success and for Hearts to find someone who fitted Craig Levein's requirements looked like being a minor miracle.

One afternoon in July 2002 a tall, heavy-boned guy turned up at Tynecastle. He reminded me of Otis Redding but this was no soul singer. It soon transpired that this handsome dude was here for a medical, not an audition. Here was the new striker, a Dutchman with a flavour of South America about him – Surinam in fact. He had good conversational English, which was a big plus for me because in the treatment room it is often important to engage the injured player in a little light discussion in order to relax him. The value of a mind and body approach to healing was borne out in my work again and again.

When the pre-season training started it became obvious that Mark De Vries was not cut out for the running side of the beautiful game. Hamstring problems arose but the lesions proved difficult to locate. In such a situation, it is difficult to not think the worst. When things which should be straightforward turn out to be irregular, alarm bells go off.

A pre-season trip to Finland had been organised to enable the team to relax and allow their strength to return after two weeks of slogging round municipal playing fields. We were based in the coastal town of Turku, the home of the famous distance runner Paavo Nurmi. Overlooking the harbour was a sculpture of him in full flight – stark naked! It brought to mind David Coleman's memorable description of the Cuban 400/800 metre runner Alberto Juantorena at the Montreal Olympics: 'He opened his legs and showed his class.'

The weather in Finland was very hot and the nights were short in the land of the midnight sun. However the training facilities were excellent and medical clinics were 'walk up'. If someone needed a scan or an X-ray it was handled on the spot, meaning that I could get an answer about a condition without trailing all over the city.

Mark remained a non-starter, although his legs were scanned with negative results. Somewhat worryingly, his contribution in training was to jog at snail's pace around the perimeter of the field. Neil Sneddon, our masseur, must have been 'weel sick' of big Mark's backside and hamstrings by the end of the tour, as massage was about all we could do.

The other newcomer was Kevin Twaddle, a wide right player who succeeded in becoming *hors de combat* after ten minutes in our first tour match. In the same game Neil Janczyk went down with sunstroke. The venue, in a forest clearing, offered little chance of shade and lavatory 'facilities' were somewhere in the woods. In the other two matches it was still no show from Mark. With the season looming large, a lot of my work with him was focused on the psychological aspects of injury but I have to say that, much as I liked the lad, conversation between physio and player was drying up.

On the flight home, we were halfway to Copenhagen in a very small aircraft when it was struck by lightning. It happened so quickly there was no panic, although when the drinks trolley appeared, fitness coach Tom Ritchie and I had a couple of large ones.

Back on terra firma, there was no rush to judgement on Mark. Thank goodness for a sympathetic manager. I have known one or two

De Vries strikes for goal against Sunderland FC, 2003.
© Eric McCowat Sports Photo Archive.

who, when they sign a new player, want to see him in training and in competition regardless of any problems he might be having.

When the season opened, the Jambos travelled to Dens Park, a notoriously difficult venue where winning the toss was often crucial, as the home team enjoyed kicking down the slope in the second half. I was always happier across the road at Tannadice. The balance of power had shifted in the City of Discovery in favour of the 'Arabs' (United's street name, perhaps deriving from the city being twinned with Nablus), making Hearts the underdogs when we visited. To scrape a draw was not a bad outcome, whereas at Dens we were expected to do better and often did not. The weight of favouritism can be a burden for some teams, while others, like the Old Firm, are used to this pressure week in, week out and handle it positively.

Mark was on the bench for the first outing of the campaign and looked on from the sidelines as the Jambos were pegged back to 1-1 with 20 minutes to go. Dundee's centre back Lee Wilkie was causing havoc at set pieces as he was a big lad with a good leap. The manager must have sensed his new arrival would like a taste of the action and he was introduced to counter Wilkie's aerial threat. This low key debut was maybe what the big Dutchman had secretly intended for himself. It paid off as he inspired the defence to a successful rearguard action. Alan Maybury, Hearts right back on the day, remembers the ground shaking when Mark arrived in the box, like the cavalry, and admitted he was delighted to have him on *his* side.

This cameo performance put some of my fears to rest. Mark had survived the introduction to life in the SPL without any apparent damage. Would there be a reaction the following morning? There wasn't, and now everyone at Tynecastle could look forward to the big man getting on the end of crosses from Jean-Louis Valois. Valois' signing reflected the manager's penchant for having a flutter and this Gallic winger proved to be as enigmatic as Mona Lisa's smile.

Edinburgh derby matches are unpredictable, results may not run to form with fairly frequent high-scoring orgies occurring – I should know, having sat through every one of them for 23 years. Hearts had recently been tanned 6-2 at Easter Road. This left a massive scar on the collective psyche at Tynecastle, and even though the man at the helm for this match had left the club, his successor would have to deal with an inherited monkey for his back. Prior to one derby the boss had hired a magician and a stand-up comedian to fill in the time between the pre-match and the game. After the ensuing defeat, the press had a field day when they got wind of this cabaret.

The strike partnership for this first derby of the season was going to be De Vries and Kirk. 'Ulster Andy' had been brought over by Jefferies and Brown two seasons earlier and I was impressed with his physique when I got a look at him at Il Ciocco, Tuscany, where we went for pre-season training. He was quick and had a great physical 'cut' to him, but any striker during that period had the spectre of John Robertson haunting him in the same way that Donald Ford and Drew Busby had the shadow of Willie Bauld to contend with during their careers. Comparisons are, as they say, odious. Enjoy the players for their talent during the times in which they live is what I say.

Bobby Williamson's Hibs team arrived at Tynecastle having had their hosts watched the week before. His scouts would have had nothing to report except for the brief appearance of a big, lumbering Dutchman who had done nothing exceptional. It's not uncommon for new signings to score in their first derby match but when Kirky broke the deadlock, few inside Tynecastle that afternoon could have been prepared for what unfolded. Mark did the rest in the second half: he blasted his way into Gorgie folklore with *four* goals, all striker's goals inside the box. The 6-2 defeat had been gloriously avenged after two years of pain. One of the little quirks of the day was the award of the Man of the Match to Jean-Louis Valois for his dashing wing play, selected *before* the last two goals went in. Not that any Jambo would begrudge him this honour but goals assume a greater significance when scored against our neighbours – much of the reverence bestowed on JR was due to his astonishing record against the Hibees. Other 'foreigners' – Foster, Musemic, Stamp, McKenna, Kirk, Quitongo, Juanjo, Kisnorbo and now, De Vries – will be remembered in Gorgie for these particular moments.

In football, clichés abound. 'It never rains but it pours' means that when things go wrong, they are likely to go wrong for a considerable time. So it was to be when Livingston gave John Robertson a job. Hearts had a big striker, Livi had a big centre half, Marvin Andrews! Mark was full of confidence since his successful start to the season but coming up against Andrews was another step up the learning curve of Scottish football.

In the first half at Almondvale, Mark took a battering which affected him mentally as well as physically. Andrews had administered the classic ploy of unscrupulous centre backs, the knee into the mid-buttock, or sacroiliac joint, which connects the pelvis to the spine and has very little muscle cover. Consequently blows are often painful and disabling.

At half time Mark was in tears. The management handled the situation well and after a restoration job by Craig and Peter, he went out for the second half, but the game ended in a win for the home side. This was the start of a run of victories for the West Lothian outfit against the Hearts. The only comfort I derived from this 'grannying', ie four wins out of four, came from the fact that JR gained some coaching kudos from the wins against his former club.

Mark did get over this clash and his goals in Europe guaranteed Hearts a place in the group stages of the 2004 UEFA Cup. Before the second match against the Portuguese side Braga, a crucial match if Hearts were to progress in the competition, he injured his foot and it was odds against him playing. He took no part in the training the night before the match and the vibes coming from the big man were not positive. I spent the next afternoon with him, trying out various taping techniques and orthotic supports. An acceptable combination of pills, injections and tapings was found which at least helped Mark's frame of mind, if not his body. As every good Jambo knows, he played, scoring two goals which meant an aggregate score of 5-3. Race horses often run better when a goat or a donkey travels with them. Perhaps the doctor and I were the human equivalents of these companions for Mark, in that his mind became composed, which in turn reduced the negative input from his foot injury – leading to a winning performance.

On 21 October Hearts had an away fixture against one of the better Dutch sides, Feyenoord. To get anything out of the tie would be a tall order and Levein would have to have his best 11 available, so it was a concern when, the week before the match in Rotterdam, Mark developed a sore big toe. There was nothing to see but it was a different story the next day. Traumatic problems don't always worsen but infections certainly do. Mark was prescribed some very strong medication – cellulitis was suspected, a very dangerous condition which can lead to septicaemia. The medication did not control Mark's infection and he had to be admitted to the Western General Hospital where intravenous antibiotics were administered. After discharge it was decided to take him to Holland to give him every chance of participating but we knew it was going to be nip and tuck whether he would be fit enough to play. This meant some serious work for Dr Melvin as the drugs were still being administered via his veins, but it was all to no avail. He couldn't play. This infection spelt the beginning of the end for Mark at Hearts and he was soon to follow his manager to Leicester City, where he flourished briefly.

CHAPTER 17

Last Bus from Gorgie

IT WAS A WONDERFUL surprise to be awarded a testimonial dinner by the Federation of Hearts Supporters Clubs. Gary Mackay, the driving force behind the event, had noticed I had been around Hearts for 20 years. Touched as I was by the occasion, the evening set the clock ticking on my time at Tynecastle as it made me ponder how long I could continue as the club physiotherapist. My parents must have passed on good health genes to me as I was rarely sick from the time I left the NHS until I gave the club my notice to quit three years after this fine evening.

I had been with Heart of Midlothian through times of momentous change. Whether or not 'Academy' is an appropriate term for a training headquarters is debatable, but to my mind Chris Robinson deserves no end of praise for the deal he cut with Heriot-Watt University. The match and training pitches, which included indoor and outdoor artificial surfaces, allowed coaches of all stripes to have a fixed base. No longer would a van have to be loaded with training paraphernalia in all weathers, then be driven to parks or school playing fields with tricky surfaces which could, as I well know, prevent the flow of play and lead to injuries. Leaving the cosy but sometimes less than pristine conditions of Tynecastle, save, perhaps, for match days, was a wrench for most of us but the management of change could be a welcome challenge.

Interestingly, Craig Levein who, in his playing prime, had embraced the effective but unscientific training methods of McNeil and Logan, completely rejected their implementation when we moved to the Riccarton campus. My expectation was that he would at least retain the speed ball as a useful distraction for injured players. But no – the

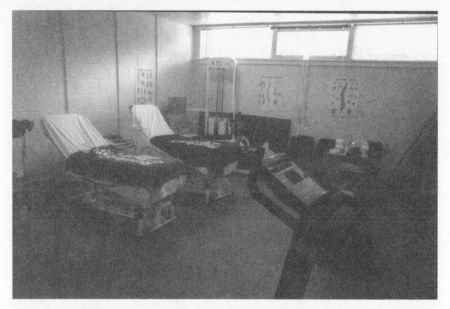

The Hearts Academy physiotherapy room at Heriot-Watt University Riccarton campus.

baby went out with the bath water. Strength and conditioning regimes were going to be the responsibility of the Sports Science Department.

Undercurrents about negotiations for the takeover of the club affected that season. The idea of moving to Murrayfield in any shape or form alienated a large section of the Gorgie faithful and perhaps this discontent was the clincher for Robinson. Although there is no denying he had moved the Hearts on during his tenure, he was always dogged by controversy. From the sacking of Sandy Clark to the changing of the Heart of Midlothian badge, he somehow weathered the many storms. For a chief executive in any business, ten or so years is a long time.

Waiting in the wings was a well-to-do, Russian-born Lithuanian businessman who had unleashed his observers on Hearts. After a Rangers game at Tynecastle, I noticed two of these henchmen exiting the grandstand *literally* rubbing their hands, and that's when I knew the Lithuanians were hot for the deal. About the same time, while in the middle of a European campaign, came Levein's move south to Leicester City. He had, correctly, sniffed the wind of change. But the Midlands club was not flowing with milk and honey, as he was to find out, the 'Foxes' having to compete with a huge following dedicated to watching 30 guys fat-arsing around with a giant suppository.

With the appointment of John Robertson as manager in November 2004 there came, inevitably, player unrest and in mid-season JR had to contend with some of the squad hoping their former gaffer might take them down to play in the more lucrative Championship. Somewhat disconcertingly from a personal perspective, all the while Lithuanian advisors were inspecting every aspect of the club. One guy, who looked like a creation out of a Hammer horror movie, appeared unannounced almost on a daily basis in the physiotherapy clinic. He would look around the place without a word, tighten the bolt through his neck and then leave.

Frustrations on the rehabilitation front began to accumulate. Foreign players would return from representing their countries with injuries acquired from sitting in economy class on long flights. Dissatisfaction with their lot was often manifested in fictional or trivial problems, just enough to rule them out of selection for the first team. When players' minds are elsewhere they are just a waste of space. Managers are not psychologists and usually the player with a grievance finds himself training with the youths. Lithuanian players, after injury, would disappear to a multi-disciplinary clinic in Germany and while this reduced my workload, it did nothing for my self-esteem.

John Robertson and Donald Park did their level best in their short tenure. A historically splendid victory in Basle in the UEFA Cup was cancelled by defeats at Murrayfield from Schalke of Germany and the Hungarian outfit Ferencváros as Hearts struggled to escape from their group. The club should have made money from this extended run in Europe but it was all rather disappointing. One of the highlights (and there were few) which I found hilarious was Robbo's frustrations boiling over and the Hungarian coach Csaba László (who would later manage Hearts) receiving a well-directed size nine in his backside.

In the league I was beginning to see decent players doing things on the pitch which were out of character, another thing which didn't sit comfortably with me. With the season coming to an end, it was obvious that JR would need a pre-season with the players he wanted to keep and those who could be promoted from the youths. There was unlikely to be any doubt in his mind that money would be required to bring in players of his choosing.

It was not to be. John and Donald left, thoroughly scunnered – I think. Now the club was faced with the reality of at least three managers within a year and that was the point at which I submitted my notice. A month would have been sufficient but I thought three would give the club time to appoint a new manager – and, when it came up their back, my successor.

As we all know, George Burley was the next occupant of the Tynecastle hot seat, and while his tenure began in the most exhilarating fashion, I had the feeling that nothing at Hearts would measure up to his standards. He was particularly critical of the youngsters and for me this was a guarded slap at Academy director John Murray, U19s coach John McGlynn and Stevie Frail.

There were many established players on their way: Kevin McKenna and Patrick Kisnorbo with their economy class problems; Alan Maybury caught the Leicester bus with big Mark De Vries as, eventually, did Joe Hamill. To replace them, three talented Czechs arrived: Roman Bednár, Michal Pospišil and the crowd-pleasing Rudi Skácel.

The first team squad clearly relished the new training regime, responding to Burley's methods in fine fashion and we headed off to the Emerald Isle to begin preparations for the new season. Having our own bus and driver got us off to a good start in Dublin and with excellent weather, dry and warm but not scorching like some of the areas Hearts had chosen in previous years, team spirit was high.

The trip was marred, though, when Graham Weir suffered a broken leg against St Patrick's Athletic, a tackle from behind leaving the striker in agony. It occurred on the same Sunday as a final of a major hurling competition and what a sight met us as we arrived at A&E with the team bus – everybody and their dogs seemed to be there with everything from hernias to hangovers. Of course Graham had more than just a common or garden fracture; it had to be one of the rare varieties which had the consultant reaching for his text book. Fortunately, surgery was not required, but Graham would have a hard start to the season as he would lose all the conditioning he had acquired from the previous weeks' hard graft – and I knew I wouldn't be around to see him through his rehab.

After a trip to Hull where Hearts played at City's splendid new stadium, the season started with a fine 4-2 win at Rugby Park. The Jambos were looking good and a convincing 4-0 Tynecastle triumph over our neighbours the following weekend kept the pot boiling nicely. The sun was shining in Gorgie but setting on my career there. Despite the team riding high at the top of the SPL thanks to a marvellous opening to the 2005–06 season and a new ambitious owner in charge, nothing was going to make me change my mind. After a narrow home win against Motherwell made possible by a remarkable last-minute save by Craig Gordon, I walked out of Tynecastle for the last time on 27 August 2005. It was time to go.

Twenty-three years of Saturday afternoons had passed in a blink. The club had been great for me, and I would like to think I had been good for Heart of Midlothian.

FRONT VIEW OF HUMAN SKELETON WITH SKIN CONTOUR

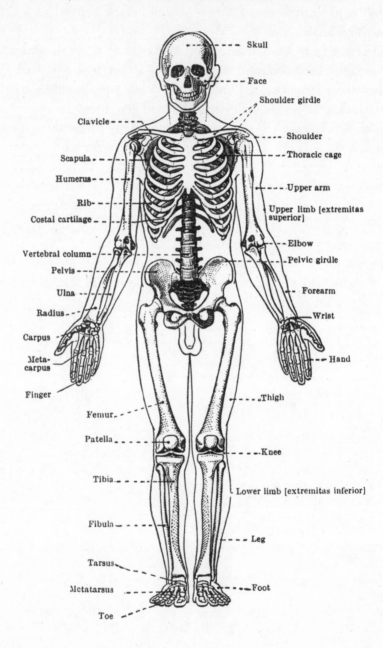

Skull

Face

Shoulder girdle

Clavicle

Shoulder

Scapula

Thoracic cage

Humerus

Upper arm

Rib

Upper limb [extremitas superior]

Costal cartilage

Elbow

Vertebral column

Pelvic girdle

Pelvis

Ulna

Forearm

Radius

Wrist

Carpus

Meta-carpus

Hand

Finger

Thigh

Femur

Patella

Knee

Tibia

Lower limb [extremitas inferior]

Fibula

Leg

Tarsus

Metatarsus

Foot

Toe

The Basic Management of Football Injuries

ANATOMICAL TERMS (POSITIONAL)

anterior = front; posterior = back; lateral = outside; medial = inside; superior = above; inferior = below.

LOWER LIMB JOINTS AND THEIR PRINCIPAL MOVEMENTS

FOOT: All phalanges flex and extend. Adduction and abduction are possible in some individuals. The phalanges also extend and flex in their articulation with the metatarsal bones. The metatarsal bones articulate proximally with the tarsal bones – these joints are very tightly bound by small ligaments in order that the arches of the foot do not collapse. As a result, individual movements are difficult to demonstrate actively.

ANKLE JOINT: This is formed by the tibia and fibula of the leg and talus bone of the foot. Upward movement of the foot on the leg (dorsiflexion) and downward movement of the same (plantar flexion) are the chief movements in this joint.

EVERSION AND INVERSION: These are two movements which occur inferiorly to the ankle joint but are closely associated with it. Injuries to the ankle region nearly always involve inversion and eversion.

KNEE JOINT: This is the largest weight-bearing joint in the body. It is formed between the lower end of the femur and the upper end of the tibia. The main movements are flexion and extension with some degree of medial and lateral rotation. The joint between the tibia and fibula is tightly bound and very little movement occurs here, however it can be manipulated to assist recovery from lateral knee joint sprains.

PATELLOFEMORAL JOINT: The patella is a sesamoid bone set into the tendon of the quadriceps mainly to facilitate the slide of the tendon over the front of the most important joint for football players. The posterior aspect of this small bone is complex and is often a source of irritation in middle and long distance runners.

HIP JOINT: This is the best example of a ball and socket joint in the human anatomy. It is formed by the head of the femur meeting with a socket on the pelvis called the acetabulum. This joint is very stable. The structure of the joint permits more movements than any of the others previously mentioned. They are flexion, extension, adduction, abduction, circumduction and rotation, both medial and lateral.

UPPER LIMB JOINTS AND THEIR PRINCIPAL MOVEMENTS

SHOULDER JOINT: This is also a ball and socket joint. However it is far less stable than the hip joint and requires strong muscles around it to keep it from dislocating when stressed in sport or heavy manual work. It is made up by the head of the humerus and a shallow cup on the scapula called the glenoid cavity.

ACROMIOCLAVICULAR JOINT: This consists of the acromion process on the scapula being bound to the lateral end of the clavicle. Downward blows on this joint or falls on the point of the shoulder often lead to small fractures or a dislocation but they are more often seen in rugby than in football.

ELBOW JOINT: Three bones are involved here; the humerus (the bones of the upper arm), and the ulna and the radius (the two bones of the forearm). The joint between the humerus and the ulna is rather like a hook or a short hinge, the ulna 'hooking' the lower end of the humerus. The joint between the radius and the humerus is not as stable as its partner, its movements however are more subtle, involving a rotation which enables the hand and forearm to be pronated and supinated; strictly speaking this is not a pure elbow movement. The movements which take place at the elbow joint are flexion and extension.

WRIST JOINT: Formed by the radius, scaphoid, lunate and triquetral bones, this is an extremely mobile area. The movements are flexion, extension, adduction (ulnar deviation), abduction (radial deviation) and circumduction.

FIRST CARPOMETACARPAL JOINT: The base of the thumb. The wide range of movement here is due to the shape of the joint surfaces. All movements including rotation and circumduction.

FIRST METACARPOPHALANGEAL JOINT: The middle joint of the thumb. The movements are the same as described for the first carpometacarpal joint – without rotation.

THE SPINE

This acts as a fairly rigid pillar which supports the upper body and protects the spinal cord and the nerves which arise from it. It consists of seven cervical, twelve thoracic and five lumbar vertebrae jointed one on top of the other. It is similar to other peripheral joints, supported by muscles and ligaments. The sacrum is made up of five fused vertebrae. Rotation, flexion, side flexion and extension are all easily demonstrated. Intervertebral discs are made of laminated cartilage and have a soft centre which occasionally protrudes causing pressure on the spinal cord or nerve roots. This is commonly known as a slipped disc.

FIGURE I – MUSCLES OF THIGH AND LEG, ANTERIOR ASPECT

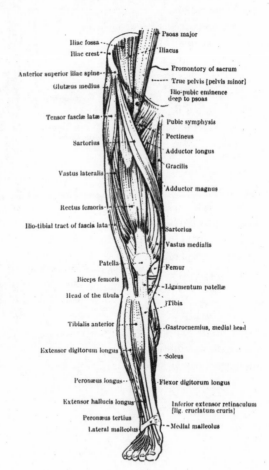

PSOAS: flexes thigh on trunk – medially rotates thigh.

QUADRICEPS (4)

RECTUS FEMORIS: flexes thigh on trunk; extends leg on thigh.

VASTUS MEDIALIS, LATERALIS, INTERMEDIUS: all extend leg on thigh.

SARTORIUS: helps to flex the knee and also brings the lower leg into the 'squat' or 'cross leg' position.

TIBIALIS ANTERIOR: Supports the medial arch of foot and dorsi flexes and inverts the ankle.

Labels on figure:

Iliac fossa
Iliac crest
Anterior superior iliac spine
Glutæus medius
Tensor fasciæ latæ
Sartorius
Vastus lateralis
Rectus femoris
Ilio-tibial tract of fascia lata
Patella
Biceps femoris
Head of the fibula
Tibialis anterior
Extensor digitorum longus
Peronæus longus
Extensor hallucis longus
Peronæus tertius
Lateral malleolus

Psoas major
Iliacus
Promontory of sacrum
True pelvis [pelvis minor]
Ilio-pubic eminence deep to psoas
Pubic symphysis
Pectineus
Adductor longus
Gracilis
Adductor magnus
Sartorius
Vastus medialis
Femur
Ligamentum patellæ
Tibia
Gastrocnemius, medial head
Soleus
Flexor digitorum longus
Inferior extensor retinaculum [lig. cruciatum cruris]
Medial malleolus

FIGURE 2 – MUSCLES OF THIGH AND LEG, POSTERIOR ASPECT

GLUTEUS MAXIMUS:
Extends the thigh.
Maintains the lower
trunk in upright
position.

HAMSTRING (3):

SEMITENDINOSUS,
SEMIMEMBRANOSUS,
BICEPS FEMORIS: All
flex the leg on the
thigh, all extend the
thigh on the trunk
(pelvis). Biceps is also
a strong lateral rotator.

GASTROCNEMIUS:

Main connection
with the Achilles
tendon; lifts the body
mass upwards (and
forwards) by plantar
flexing the foot.

SOLEUS: Involved
mainly in maintaining
the leg on the foot in
standing.

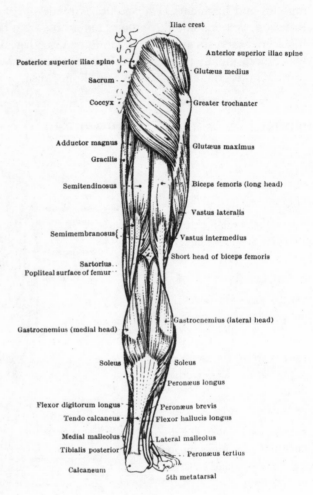

FIGURE 3 – INNER (MEDIAL) THIGH AND LEG

The main muscles here are the adductors which hold the leg in the midline position or pull the limb medially from an abducted position. Note where they are attached to the pelvis.

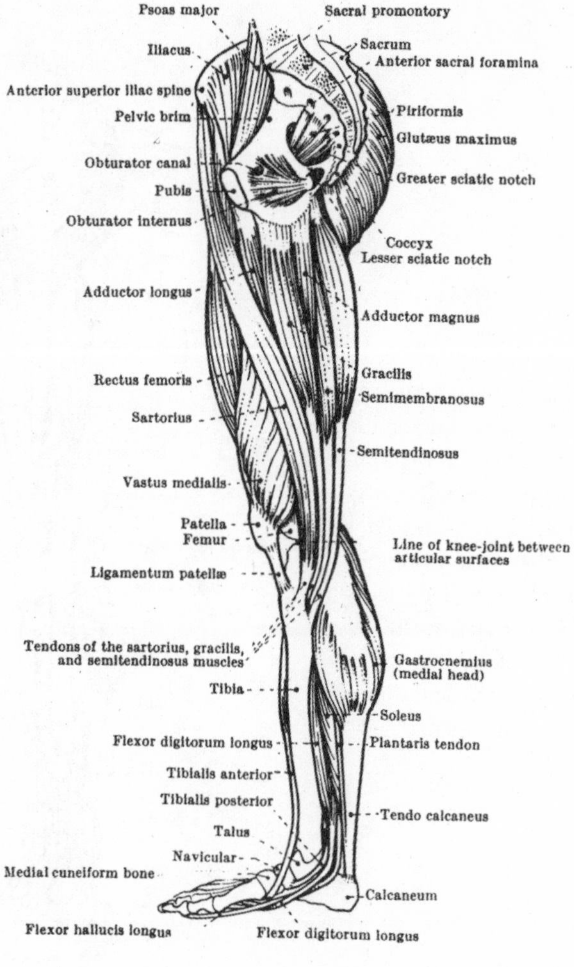

Psoas major
Sacral promontory
Iliacus
Sacrum
Anterior sacral foramina
Anterior superior iliac spine
Pelvic brim
Piriformis
Glutæus maximus
Obturator canal
Greater sciatic notch
Pubis
Obturator internus
Coccyx
Lesser sciatic notch
Adductor longus
Adductor magnus
Rectus femoris
Gracilis
Semimembranosus
Sartorius
Semitendinosus
Vastus medialis
Patella
Femur
Line of knee-joint between articular surfaces
Ligamentum patellæ
Tendons of the sartorius, gracilis, and semitendinosus muscles
Gastrocnemius (medial head)
Tibia
Soleus
Flexor digitorum longus
Plantaris tendon
Tibialis anterior
Tibialis posterior
Tendo calcaneus
Talus
Navicular
Medial cuneiform bone
Calcaneum
Flexor hallucis longus
Flexor digitorum longus

FIGURE 4 – OUTER (LATERAL) THIGH AND LEG

Iliac crest
Anterior superior iliac spine
Glutæus medius
Glutæus maximus
Sartorius
Tensor fasciæ latæ
Greater trochanter
Rectus femoris
Cut edge of ilio-tibial tract of fascia lata
Long head of biceps femoris
Ilio-tibial tract
Short head
Vastus lateralis
Femur
Vastus intermedius
Interarticular line of knee-joint
Patella
Ligamentum patellæ
Head of fibula
Tubercle [tuberosity] of tibia
Gastrocnemius, lateral head
Tibialis anterior
Soleus
Extensor digitorum longus
Peronæus longus
Peronæus brevis
Tendo calcaneus
Peronæus tertius
Extensor hallucis longus
Lateral malleolus
Calcaneum
Cuboid
5th metatarsal
Extensor digitorum brevis

Figure 4 shows the outer hamstring and its attachment to the fibula. The peroneal muscles which control the lateral ankle area are shown to good effect. They evert the foot and dorsiflex the ankle. When the ankle is 'turned' they are often damaged.

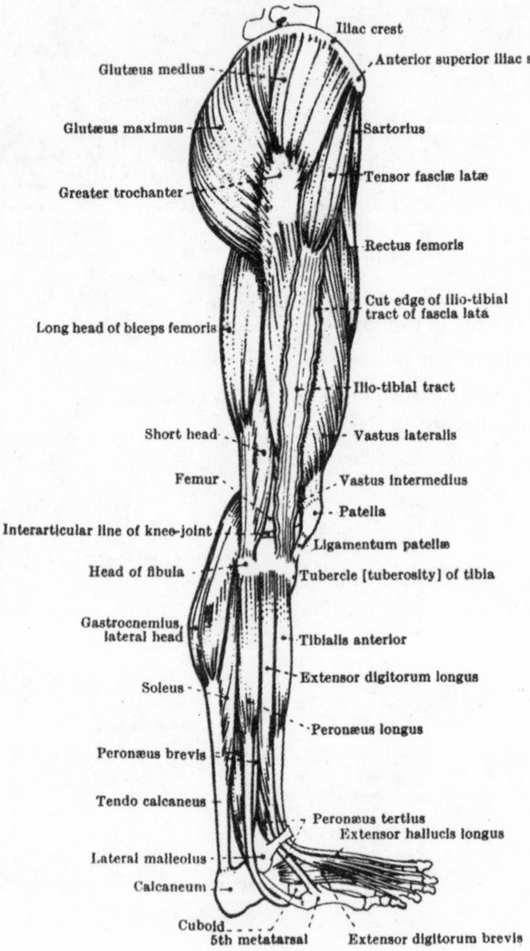

174

FIGURE 5 – ANTERIOR TRUNK

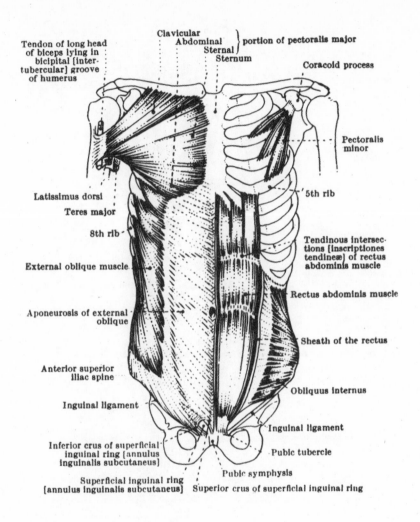

The attachments of the abdominal
muscles to the pelvis support the
spine (from the front) and protect the
abdominal organs. The rectus abdominis
muscle flexes the trunk on the thigh.

FIGURE 6 – POSTERIOR MUSCLES OF TRUNK

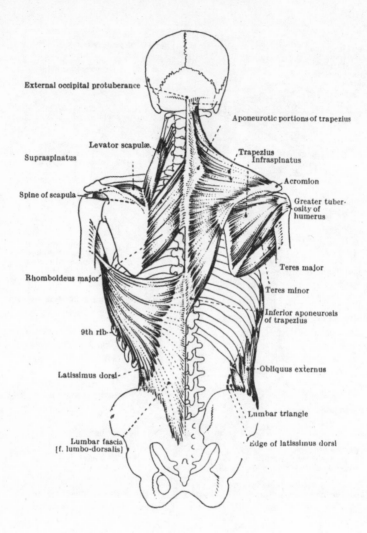

External occipital protuberance

Aponeurotic portions of trapezius

Levator scapulæ

Trapezius
Infraspinatus

Supraspinatus

Acromion

Spine of scapula

Greater tuberosity of humerus

Teres major

Rhomboideus major

Teres minor

Inferior aponeurosis of trapezius

9th rib

Latissimus dorsi

Obliquus externus

Lumbar triangle

Lumbar fascia
[f. lumbo-dorsalis]

Edge of latissimus dorsi

For footballers the trapezius, which
supports the shoulder girdle and
protects the spine at the neck, is the
most important of the posterior muscles
of the trunk.

FIGURE 7 – MUSCLES OF UPPER LIMB – ANTERIOR ASPECT

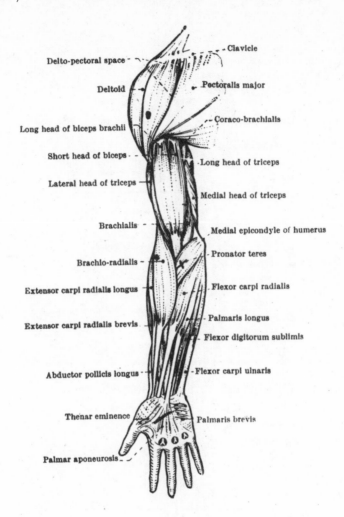

For goalkeepers the deltoid muscles should be strengthened to protect the shoulder joint, which depends on soft tissue for stability. The deltoid abducts, flexes and extends the upper limb.

FIGURE 8 – MUSCLES OF UPPER LIMB – POSTERIOR ASPECT

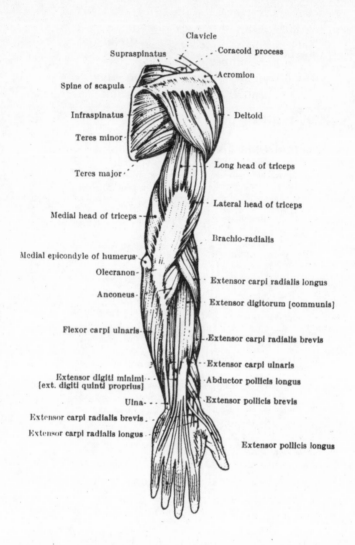

This figure shows the origin of the
forearm muscles – often a source of
irritation in golfers and tennis players.

COMMON FOOTBALL INJURIES

Most injuries present with one or more of these signs of inflammation: pain, swelling, redness, heat. Most are caused by overuse or direct trauma. Where there has been internal bleeding, lower limb elevation, post-injury, is essential. Rest, ice and compression all help, but resting in elevation for eight hours at night should be stressed to all injured players. The following, taken together, will indicate the severity of the injury: site, size, symptoms.

THE FEET

HALLUX VALGUS: Caused by an imbalance in the small muscles of the feet and/or tight footwear. Apart from surgery there is no effective treatment. A boot stretcher can be used to alleviate pressure over the swollen joint. Chiropodists may suggest toe spacers, which may be of some value when the condition is acute.

HALLUX RIGIDUS: The acute phase of this painful condition can be treated with ice to the affected joint, the first metatarsophalangeal joint, and gentle mobilising non-weight-bearing exercises.

TAILOR'S BUNION: Worthy of mention as the immobility of the joint at the base of the fifth toe often leads to a fungal infection in the web space between the fourth and fifth toe, this is due to lack of hygiene and inadequate drying after bathing.

PLANTAR FASCIITIS: Often caused by a change in running activities or playing surfaces. The main problem is located along the medial, plantar surface of the foot. This condition may take three to four weeks to clear. A strapping with felt support is often helpful.

There are many conditions around the heel bone (calcaneum), some caused by repeated trauma to the sole of the heel, others by the pull of the Tendo Achilles on the heel bone. Small bony spurs may be seen on X-ray. These may settle with rest or respond to an anti-inflammatory injection.

SEVER'S DISEASE: Occasionally seen in children aged 10–14, affecting the growing heel bone. No treatment available other than six weeks' to three months' rest.

BURSITIS: these are inflamed pads of fat which normally allow tendons to pass over the bone without friction. Often this bursa between the Achilles tendon and the heel bone may become irritated due to ill-fitting shoes etc.

STRESS FRACTURE: This is usually a metatarsal bone. When it occurs, the player will have some pain and be unable to bear weight on the foot. X-rays do not always show this fracture immediately. If the first X-ray is negative and the symptoms have persisted, a repeat picture after two weeks may show the fracture, as there will be evidence of bone activity by then.

FRACTURE OF THE BASE OF THE FIFTH METATARSAL (JONES FRACTURE): This often occurs when the ankle is turned. A violent contraction of the peroneal muscles combined with the turn may fracture the base of this little bone. Without rest in plaster, healing is less likely to happen. An inability to bear weight through the foot should be taken as a sign that something serious is wrong.

PULP CAVITY INFECTION: This can be caused in either the pads of the fingers or toes by a pin-prick infection. It is an extremely painful condition which does not necessarily show all the cardinal signs of inflammation until the patient is quite ill. Strong antibiotics and minor surgery are required.

AVULSION FRACTURE: Occurs when a tendon responds to a strong muscle contraction by pulling off the piece of bone to which it is attached, most often where the tendon of peroneus brevis attaches to the fifth metatarsal.

THE ANKLE AND SUBTALAR JOINTS

FOOTBALLER'S ANKLE: This condition is most often seen in the dominant foot. The bone along the anterior joint line becomes irritated by repeated minor trauma. In response, the body produces more bone; the excess often breaks off and may drift into the joint, causing a 'locked' feeling and acute discomfort in the joint. Rest from activity and a small heel-raise worn for a short period may help the condition to settle. In extreme cases surgery may may be required to remove the loose bodies from the joint.

INVERSION INJURY: Damage to medial and lateral structures around the ankle is common amongst players of ball games. During recovery the muscles which support the ankle become weak and desensitised to postural demands. Unless this is recognised re-injury is likely. Early mobilisation is essential when there is no bone or severe ligamentous damage. The player should be encouraged to walk normally and perform non-weight-bearing exercises. Simple flexion and extension are beneficial in the first ten days. Strapping and canvas ankle braces are useful when training resumes. Balance training is essential to resensitise the musculature supporting the ankle.

EVERSION INJURY: This frequently occurs when a tackle or control of a driven ball is mistimed. The foot levers the medial aspect of the ankle open further than normal, spraining the anteromedial aspect of the joint. In severe cases the medial collateral ligament of the knee may be involved. A firm strapping applied after the first 72 hours have passed may allow the player to train and play, given a positive approach to the game.

PLANTAR FLEXION INJURY: When a player kicks the sole of an opponent's boot, the foot is forcibly driven into plantar flexion – much further than normal. The 'nipping' effect on the posterior aspect of the ankle is painful. It limits activity and is very difficult to treat. An X-ray should be considered, in case there is a minor fracture of the talus.

AVULSION FRACTURES: These are fairly common around the anteromedial and lateral aspects of the ankle. The small ligaments, when stressed, often pull fragments of bone away rather than themselves tearing. Instability in an ankle manifests in a limping, partial weight-bearing gait. A resting plaster for ten days to three weeks is often the preferred course of action.

MAJOR FRACTURES: These are usually unmistakeable, however the fibula may be fractured above the ankle without being diagnosed at first examination. Stress fractures of the tibia have been known to go undiagnosed.

THE KNEE JOINT

This is the largest joint in the body. It is held together by four main ligaments, the medial collateral, the lateral, the anterior cruciate and the posterior cruciate ligaments. The muscles protecting the integrity of the knee are the quadriceps and hamstrings. If there is a weakness in any of these seven muscles then the knee will be at risk in body contact sports.

1. A puffy swelling which can be moved from one side of the joint to the other manually is an indication of internal joint damage to the medial cartilage and/or the anterior cruciate ligament.

Blows or collisions involving a force moving the thigh from medial to lateral will threaten or damage the medial collateral ligament and/or medial meniscus and/or the anterior cruciate ligament.

2. Sprain of the MCL usually takes six weeks to rehabilitate in non-professional players. Non-weight-bearing quads exercises are essential in the first three weeks. These must be performed with conviction.

3. A tear in the middle of the meniscus will never heal; surgery is required to remedy the problem.

4. A damaged anterior cruciate ligament may take nine months to one year to improve. Caution is required, particularly when there is loss of full extension, an inability to squat on the affected leg and a subjective feeling that the knee is 'not quite right'.

5. Swelling apparently associated with the knee joint may initially appear horrendous. On asking the player to perform a few functions it may become clear that the joint is sound and that most of the swelling is related to a blow which did not involve rotation or twisting of the joint.

ACHILLES TENDON PROBLEMS: Irritation of this particular strong tendon may result in a chronic inflammation which is quite disabling and may lead to an eventual rupture. The player should rest completely from training and competition for a minimum of three weeks. A light plaster is sometimes applied to ensure that rest is complete. One of the significant symptoms of Achilles tendon injury is early morning stiffness, ie when the player gets out of bed the tendon will be stiff and painful for the first two steps. Until this symptom disappears training should not be attempted.

CALF MUSCLES TEARS: More common in gymnasium five-a-sides where firm surfaces are the norm. The tear usually occurs where the muscle on the medial aspect of the calf blends with the tendon. These tears are painful for three to five days. A substantial heel raise will facilitate walking. Graduated exercises usually begin after ten days.

THIGH MUSCLE TEARS: Experience of anterior thigh injuries suggests that it is mainly the rectus femoris which is involved. It is because this is an explosive muscle working over the hip and thigh that it takes so long to heal. The answer is usually six weeks' complete rest but it is not unknown for a tear in this area to be troublesome for nine months. Apart from advice and guidance, physiotherapy is usually directed at the body as a whole while this wearisome condition heals.

HAMSTRING PROBLEMS: These muscles are of the two-joint variety; they are dynamic and explosive but not as strong individually or collectively as the quadriceps. They progressively shorten through life. All players should be able to attain a stretch of 90 degrees, ie flexion of an extended lower limb on a supine trunk. An inadequate stretch of hamstrings will lead to lower back pain and an eventual tear in one of the three muscles in the group. Major tears which feel like a blow from a club in the back of the thigh will take four to eight weeks to recover. Light exercise may begin after 10–14 days. In the two previous conditions there should be a full, pain-free stretch of the muscles before training is resumed.

THE HIP JOINT: Due to its stable nature, problems in the actual joint are few in early/mid adulthood. However, range of movement in both hips should be compared one with the other in all complaints around this area. Adolescents complaining of hip pain should always be taken seriously. Growth defects do not always become apparent until the hip is subjected to stressful activity.

ADDUCTOR ATTACHMENT PAIN: The adductor muscles stabilise the thigh. They act over one joint, and are therefore less dynamic. A change of playing surface often causes pain in the upper part of these muscles. Frequently their attachment to the pelvis is damaged. Unless activities are discontinued, a long term problem may result. To keep fit while recovering from groin problems it is worthwhile 'running in water'. This involves running in the deep end of a pool. It is less stressful then running within a tolerable range on firm surfaces.

HERNIA: A hernia is a protrusion of any organ or part of an organ through the cavity which contains it. When a player complains of a lower abdominal or upper thigh pain, or both, there is a possibility that it is a hernia. A surgical opinion should be sought. Recovery from a hernia repair takes about 12 weeks. Lower back problems may cause an ache into the thigh, lateral knee joint, testicles and groin.

HAEMATOMA: This is a collection of blood which accumulates in the tissues following trauma. It is usually trapped and this is what causes the discomfort and limitation of movement. In footballers, haematomas occur mainly in the thigh, anterior, anterolateral or lateral aspects. These are either intramuscular or intermuscular.

INTRAMUSCULAR HAEMATOMAS: The bleeding is in the muscle and cannot escape. If activity continues, the condition becomes much worse, with almost immediate loss of function. There is difficulty in bending the knee; the thigh, in severe cases, has a 'wooden' feel to it and will be painful and swollen. Rest and elevation are essential. Heat, massage and exercise are contraindicated. The thigh should soften; an increase in function and a decrease in swelling should be observed after 48–72 hours. If the condition continues to worsen medical advice should be sought. Sometimes a fasciotomy is performed to relieve the pressure on nerves and blood supply.

INTERMUSCULAR HAEMATOMA: This is a bleed between muscles; the blood in such cases can disperse along the length of muscle groups. Function returns within 24 hours although a further 24 hours' rest is thought to be appropriate to ensure that the problem is inter and not intra.

SHOULDER INJURIES

Healthy functional bulk in the shoulder girdle and its main muscle groups – deltoid, trapezius, supraspinatus, biceps, triceps, pectorales major and minor – ensures that the shoulder and the acromioclavicular joints are protected. This is particularly important for goalkeepers, who land on their shoulders on all sorts of surfaces. The shoulder is a 'sloppy' ball and socket joint which relies on soft tissue to prevent subluxation, or dislocation. When a player sustains a shoulder injury and it is certain that there is no bone broken, early mobility should be pursued unless medical advice states otherwise. The player should 'grin and bear it'. Recurrent dislocation of the shoulder will nearly always require surgical repair and perhaps a year out of the game.

THE ELBOW JOINT

When injured, this joint should never be passively moved; only active exercise on the part of the player should be attempted. Myositis ossificans may result if a damaged elbow joint is mishandled: bone cells invade the surrounding muscles, rendering it immovable.

THE WRIST

Although players are always falling on outstretched hands, wrists are rarely broken, though the scaphoid bone between the wrist and the base of the thumb is sometimes broken when weight is taken through the hand. It heals slowly due to the poor circulation to the bone fragment. In some cases surgery may be required to remove necrotic bone.

THE SPINE

Neck and back pain of sudden or several hours' onset often resolves after 72 hours. Many pains and restrictions to spinal movements are stress-related.

PERIPHERAL NERVE INJURIES

Fairly rare, periperal nerve injuries may occur as a complication of another injury. Most will be temporary, causing minor weakness/paralyses. Nerves near the surface of the skin are most likely to be affected.

HEAD, TORSO AND NECK INJURIES

THE HEAD: Loss of consciousness may result in loss of life due to a respiratory arrest, an aspiration of stomach contents, or the blocking of the airway by the tongue. Getting air into the lungs is the priority. If the player is breathing, he should be placed in the recovery position. If he is not breathing, the neck should be extended and mouth-to-mouth resuscitation started. During this procedure, the player's chest should be watched to ensure that air is inflating the chest. If the chest is not moving, the mouth and back of the throat should be examined and cleared. Tilting the head back by pushing the chin may clear the airway.

THE NECK: If a player sustains a neck injury during a match and as a result has lost mobility and feeling in the arms and/or legs, qualified personnel should be sought to remove the player so that no further injury is suffered. This scenario is unlikely to happen, but it should be remembered that sparing a few minutes may save a player from a lifetime in a wheelchair.

EYES: Following a head knock it is wise to look at the eyes. If the pupil reaction is different or one is larger than the other, the player should be removed from the field. If, when checking the player later, the same problem is evident, medical examination is necessary.

ABDOMEN: Any violent blow to the upper left abdomen which shocks the player should be treated with respect. If there is no sign of recovery within 15–20 minutes he should be removed to hospital. The spleen may be ruptured.

RIBS: Broken ribs will 'click' or 'grate' under the hand where the chest is palpated. The upper seven ribs are firmest, being attached to the spine and anteriorly to the costal cartilages. Due to this stability, they are usually the most vulnerable. Occasionally the fractured rib will pierce the pleura and a collapsed lung will result. The player will obviously be in pain, breathless, and may be shocked. Removal to hospital in this case is essential. Bruised ribs may require three weeks' rest. It is worth noting that the 11th and 12th ribs – known as the 'floating ribs'– may also be fractured by a flexed knee thrust into the posterolateral loin.

THE FACE: Cuts are best compressed by a dry towel rather than a sponge. If the player is to continue, Vaseline can be used to plug the cut. Stitching should be applied earlier rather than later.

FACIAL FRACTURES: These are not uncommon. Elbows, heads, knees, feet and fists are all capable of fracturing the lower bones of the skull and face. The physio will not have to look, the player will know – if he is conscious – that something serious has occurred.

NOSE BLEEDS/BREAKS: Moderate bleeding is easily staunched by some light cotton wool in the nostril. Profuse bleeding may indicate a fracture. The player should be removed from the field – walking if possible. The nostrils can be pinched for five minutes until the bleeding stops. Damage can then be assessed. Fractures around this area should be given respect – infections which arise here are perilously close to the brain.

WHEN A PLAYER IS INJURED –

1. Observe the mechanisms of injury and the reaction of the player.
2. Listen to what the player articulates about their injury.
3. Demand a verbal response if none has been forthcoming.
5. Look – make a visual assessment.
6. Assess whether the player's reaction is lessening or worsening.
7. Notice if the limb has an unnatural appearance or swelling and whether the player has control of the injured muscle, joint etc.
8. Palpate with care the area involved.
9. Reassure the injured player.
10. Always think of damage limitation.
11. Rehabilitation begins when first aid ends.
12. Err on the side of caution. If in doubt about the player's mobility, remove the player from the field using a stretcher – there's always another game.

Note: The above text on football injuries is based on a booklet written by Alan Rae during his time as a physiotherapist at Heart of Midlothian FC and is not intended to be comprehensive in its guidance.

Index

Luath Press Limited

committed to publishing well written books worth reading

LUATH PRESS takes its name from Robert Burns, whose little collie
Luath (*Gael.*, swift or nimble) tripped up Jean Armour at a wedding
and gave him the chance to speak to the woman who was to be his wife
and the abiding love of his life. Burns called one of the 'Twa Dogs'
Luath after Cuchullin's hunting dog in Ossian's *Fingal*.
Luath Press was established in 1981 in the heart of
Burns country, and is now based a few steps up
the road from Burns' first lodgings on
Edinburgh's Royal Mile. Luath offers you
distinctive writing with a hint of
unexpected pleasures.
Most bookshops in the UK, the US, Canada,
Australia, New Zealand and parts of Europe,
either carry our books in stock or can order them
for you. To order direct from us, please send a £sterling
cheque, postal order, international money order or your
credit card details (number, address of cardholder and
expiry date) to us at the address below. Please add post
and packing as follows: UK – £1.00 per delivery address;
overseas surface mail – £2.50 per delivery address; overseas airmail
– £3.50 for the first book to each delivery address, plus £1.00 for each
additional book by airmail to the same address. If your order is a gift,
we will happily enclose your card or message at no extra charge.

Luath Press Limited
543/2 Castlehill
The Royal Mile
Edinburgh EH1 2ND
Scotland
Telephone: +44 (0)131 225 4326 (24
hours)
Fax: +44 (0)131 225 4324
email: sales@luath. co.uk
Website: www. luath.co.uk